The Endless Song

The Endless Song

**13 Lessons in
Music and Worship
of the Church**

Kenneth W. Osbeck

KREGEL PUBLICATIONS
Grand Rapids, Michigan 49501

The Endless Song, by Kenneth W. Osbeck.
Copyright © 1987 by Kregel Publications, a division of
Kregel, Inc. All rights reserved.

Unless otherwise indicated, Scripture quotations are from
the *Holy Bible,* New International Version, copyright ©
1973, 1978, 1984 by the International Bible Society. Used
by permission of Zondervan Bible Publishers.

Library of Congress Cataloging-in-Publication Data

Osbeck, Kenneth W. (1924-   )
  The Endless Song.

  Includes index.
  1. Church music.   2. Music in churches.   I. Title.
BV290.083   1987   264'.2   87-3755

ISBN 0-8254-3424-6

1 2 3 4 5 Printing/Year 91 90 89 88 87

Printed in the United States of America

DEDICATION

To Paul W. Bennehoff,
Book Editor of Kregel Publications,
longtime pastor and youth worker,
whose concern for the worship and praise of God
in the local church
has prompted the writing of this study book.

CONTENTS

PREFACE

Music enriches man's religious life. This was true when the Jewish people worshiped Jehovah in the tabernacle and temples. It was true during the early centuries of the Christian church. The music of the church was the wind that spread the flame of the Protestant Reformation. The rise of pietism and evangelicalism in the 17th and 18th centuries, with their emphasis on individual conversion and holy living, was promoted through hymns by writers such as Isaac Watts and Charles Wesley. The gospel song movement in America during the 19th century, represented by spiritual stalwarts such as D.L. Moody, Ira Sankey, and Fanny Crosby, was a powerful influence in the great evangelistic crusades.

The 20th century has witnessed an explosion in the publication and use of church music. This century has given rise to graded choirs, dramatic musicals, and the use of handbells, and orchestral-rhythm instruments. Innovations have come into the church: sound track accompaniments, electronic music, and multi-media performances.

The music of the church should involve everyone — not just a few elitist musicians. Worship and praise are predominant themes throughout the Scriptures. The gifts of voice and communication are two of God's choicest blessings to mankind. The voice lifted in praise is one of the most sublime ways mankind honors the Almighty.

In spite of its spiritual potential, music is often controversial in church life today. Tensions about appropriate musical styles and usage have long existed, but they are more prevalent and intense now than ever before. Personal preferences in the matter of traditional versus contemporary music, or in the use of amplified rhythm instruments, sound tracks, drama, choreography, or liturgical dance have produced unrest and division among believers in local churches.

As we approach these next 13 lessons let us do so with an open mind and a seeking heart. Let us ask God to give us a greater awareness of the importance of music in the church's mission. We will work to develop a biblical basis for our convictions about music, a historical perspective of the subject, a spiritual philosophy for our cultural preferences, and a genuine desire to revitalize and improve the music elements of our worship and praise.

LET EVERYTHING THAT HATH BREATH PRAISE THE LORD.

Psalm 149:1, 150:3-6

INTRODUCTION

Come, Christians, Join to Sing

Christian H. Bateman, 1843

Traditional Spanish melody

1. Come, Chris-tians, join to sing Al - le - lu - ia! A - men!
2. Come, lift your hearts on high, Al - le - lu - ia! A - men!
3. Praise yet our Christ a - gain, Al - le - lu - ia! A - men!

Loud praise to Christ our King; Al - le - lu - ia! A - men!
Let prais - es fill the sky; Al - le - lu - ia! A - men!
Life shall not end the strain; Al - le - lu - ia! A - men!

Let all, with heart and voice, Be - fore His throne re - joice;
He is our Guide and Friend; To us He'll con - de - scend;
On heav - en's bliss - ful shore His good - ness we'll a - dore,

Praise is His gra - cious choice: Al - le - lu - ia! A - men!
His love shall nev - er end: Al - le - lu - ia! A - men!
Sing - ing for - ev - er - more, "Al - le - lu - ia! A - men!"

1

THE SINGING CHRISTIAN

I will declare Your name to my brothers; in the presence of the congregation I will sing Your praises.   Hebrews 2:12

"Why do we always have to sing in church?" This pointed question was blurted out to me by a tow-headed boy who had reached a state of musical frustration during one of our children's choir rehearsals.

How would you have answered my young friend's question? It made me ask myself, "Why do we sing in church? Is it merely a way to fill the time? Has it degenerated into a routine? Is it simply a part of the preliminaries?"

As a choir director and song leader for more than 30 years, I have concluded that many Christians in our congregations share this boy's disinterest in singing. I wish you could stand with me on a church platform and watch congregations sing. I am sure you would soon agree that many Christians appear to have come to church for purposes other than having a vital encounter with God. Comparatively few seem to lose themselves in worship and praise. Others seldom give evidence of applying to themselves the great truths they are singing. How different would be our times of congregational praise if each of us would heed the apostle Paul's admonition in 1 Corinthians 14:15, "I will sing with my spirit, but I will also sing with my mind." Not everyone is able to sing tunefully, but everyone in whom the Spirit of God dwells can respond to Him with joyful praise.

> I will praise Him! I will praise Him! Praise the Lamb for sinners slain; Give Him glory, all ye people, for His blood can wash away each stain.   —Margaret J. Harris

Singing Honors God

"Why do we always have to sing in church?" One response to the youngster's question could have been this: *Singing honors God.* The psalmist David wrote, "How good it is to sing praises to our God, how pleasant and fitting to praise Him" (Psalm 147:1). Singing is a normal human response to life. It can be the mind's greatest solace and express its noblest inspiration. The activity of singing has therapeutic value for the individual who learns to enjoy it. But of far greater importance to a believer than his personal enjoyment of music is the knowledge that *when the voice is lifted in praise, God is glorified.*

"He who offers praise honors Me" (Psalm 50:23). Scripture gives amazing prominence to "praise, singing, and music." Words related to these activities appear 575 times throughout the Bible. References to music are found in 44 of the 66 books of the Bible. One entire book of 150 chapters, Psalms, is believed to have been originally a Jewish hymnbook. No one opposes the claim that of all the world's religions, only Christianity is a singing faith.

Why do we sing, my young friend? Because God has given us music to bring us pleasure. Because He has given us voices to honor Him. Let us never forget that "to glorify God and to enjoy Him forever" should be the ultimate goal of all human existence.

> To God be the glory — great things He hath done!
> So loved He the world that He gave us His Son,
> Who yielded His life an atonement for sin
> And opened the life-gate that all may go in.
> Praise the Lord!   —Fanny J. Crosby

Singing Instructs Us

I could have told my young chorister friend that *singing is a teaching and motivating device.* Have you ever considered the number of ideas and concepts (both good and bad) that come into our lives through songs? From ancient times until now, young warriors have marched away from home and loved ones, to the dangers of battle, at the call of trumpets and the roll of drums. Physicians, dentists, and therapists use the healing effects of music for easing pain and helping troubled minds. Employers have learned that music reduces the fatigue and boredom of workers and increases production. Advertisers have discovered the persuasive power of musical commercials for the sale of products.

Where did you first learn about God's concern and love for you? For many of us, it was at our mother's knee or in the Sunday School nursery, as we sang one of our first songs, "Jesus loves me, this I know, for the Bible tells me so." "Jesus loves the little children, all the children of the world — red, yellow, black and white" may have been our earliest lesson in racial understanding and missionary concern. We have learned profound spiritual truths through the songs we have learned to sing.

> Open my eyes, that I may see glimpses of truth Thou hast for me; place in my hands the wonderful key that shall unclasp and set me free. Open my eyes, ears, heart — illumine me, Spirit divine! —Clara H. Scott

Singing Encourages Us

Whenever the evil spirit from God came upon Saul, David would take his harp and play. Then relief would come to Saul; he would feel better, and the evil spirit would leave him. —1 Samuel 16:23

Many believers, like King Saul, have experienced *the healing, encouraging power of sacred song.* They have come to a church service with their hearts filled with fear and anxiety, or with their spirits drooping with an onslaught of depression. They may have experienced serious physical, financial, or emotional difficulties during the week. The daily demands of living may have built up a mountain of despondency. But then they hear a triumphant anthem of praise, a majestic hymn of worship, or a simple gospel song that reminds them of God's presence and guidance. The struggling Christians' burdens are lifted, their minds become clear, their fragile emotions are mended, and their hearts are singing once again as they return to their busy life.

At special times, a specific song will be used of God to minister to a particular spiritual need. I can recall vividly how a gospel song helped me during my first months of military service while crossing the Atlantic Ocean in a convoy during the early days of World War II. I remember standing alone on deck, communing with God through these words of song: "I trust in God wherever I may be, upon the land or on the rolling sea; and come what may from day to day, my Heavenly Father watches over me." Call this a fear neurosis if you wish; nevertheless, I learned through the message of song that God's presence is real and encouraging. I am certain that a person could find similar testimonies from many of God's people to support this axiom: *"A believer's practical theology is often his hymnology."*

I sing because I'm happy, I sing because I'm free;
For His eye is on the sparrow, and I know He watches me.
—Mrs. C.D. Martin

You are my hiding place; You will protect me from trouble and surround me with songs of deliverance.   —Psalm 32:7

For I know the plans I have for you...plans to prosper you and not to harm you, plans to give you hope and a future.
—Jeremiah 29:11

Singing Prepares Us

In answer to my young friend's question, I could also have told him that *singing prepares us for heaven.* The Bible teaches that we will enjoy giving praise and singing throughout eternity. Someone has written, "Nobody dreams of music in hell, and nobody conceives of heaven without it." The dominant theme of our endless song in heaven will likely be:

You are worthy, our Lord and God, to receive glory and honor and power, for You created all things, and by Your will they were created and have their being.   —Revelation 4:11

Do you ever let your imagination picture for you what that great day of rejoicing will be like? That day when people from every family and tribe ascribe to Him all majesty and power? That day when Christ is crowned Lord of all? When John's Isle of Patmos vision becomes reality?

After this I looked and there before me was a great multitude that no one could count, from every nation, tribe, people and language, standing before the throne and in front of the Lamb. They were wearing white robes and were holding palm branches in their hands. And they cried out with a loud voice: "Salvation belongs to our God, who sits on the throne, and to the Lamb." All the angels were standing around the throne and around the elders and the four living creatures. They fell down on their faces before the throne and worshiped God, saying: "Amen! Praise and glory and wisdom and thanks and honor and power and strength be to our God for ever and ever. Amen!"

—Revelation 7:9-12

Truly, "what a day of rejoicing that will be, when we all see Jesus, and we sing and shout the victory!" The glorious prospect of heaven should evoke this response from every believer: "O Lord Jesus how long, how long till we shout that glad song. . .?" And until that glad day, may we know the joy of glorifying God as we join our voices in praise to the One who died that we might live to sing eternally.

Come, we that love the Lord, and let our joys be known
Join in a song with sweet accord and thus surround the thone.
Then let our songs abound, and every tear be dry
We're marching through Emmanuel's ground to fairer worlds
on high.   —Isaac Watts
". . .they are the kind of worshipers the Father seeks."

—John 4:23

Singing Requires Our Stewardship

Let me warn you, however, that music has as much potential for evil as it has for good. Missionaries have spoken of the hypnotic effects of music on the people they serve. Even in our highly civilized western culture, we read and observe shocking reports of the base passions that are aroused and the shameful acts that are incited at all-night rock festivals or through the vulgar, implicit inferences of some television videos. A convincing case can be made for a correlation between many of the "top 40 songs"— with their restless rhythms, negative philosophies, and suggestive implications—and the moral decadence of today's society.

Here is how Ezekiel described Satan: "The workmanship of your timbrels and pipes was prepared for you on the day you were created" (Ezekiel 28:13, KJV). Satan was created to be an angelic being of praise and adoration to God. He was a veritable musical instrument. But he turned all that potential to himself and fell victim to his own pride and ambition. Perhaps this explains why many people are easily enthralled by sensuous music. *The result is that, rather than being a blessing to mankind, music becomes a curse.*

Consider this chilling paragraph, written by one of the last missionaries to leave the People's Republic of China. In his book, *Meditations From a Prison Cell,* missionary F. Olin Stockwell related this account:

> During the first long period of my imprisonment, I was at a center where the government was training its new cadres. The young people, seventy-five to a hundred of them at a time, were brought in and given six or eight weeks of training and indoctrination before being sent out to government jobs. The mornings were spent in study, the afternoons and evenings in singing. The leader had no instrument other than a pitch pipe. Sounding the note, he would sing a phrase. Then the group would sing it over in the same way. Thus phrase after phrase was lined off until the young people had the melody firmly in mind. After that, they memorized the words. The tunes were catchy, easy to remember. Over and over they sang these songs until the whole courtyard rang with music. In this way the hates and fears, the hope and faith of Communism sang themselves into the minds and hearts of these youth. This is being done all over China — in schools, offices, army and training groups. China is singing herself into the Communist ideology.

Summary

Singing God's praises is an evidence of a believer's true spiritual joy. Recently, I rejoiced with a person who testified that before he became a Christian, singing was foreign and even distasteful in his life. Now that he had become a believer in Christ, he enjoyed singing the praises of God and sharing a testimony in song.

The voice is truly a remarkable gift from God. It brings pleasure into our own lives, and it allows us to offer praise to our Creator. It also gives us the ability to share thoughts and feelings with others. One important argument in support of creationism — that man is the image bearer of God and not the result of mere chance evolution — is that only man has been given the ability to communicate an organized language with a voice. Even more, man can enhance his verbal and spiritual expressions with musical sounds of pitch, duration, and harmonies — HE CAN SING! *Singing, then, is a unique expression of the image of God in us.*

Music has unusual powers to influence the minds and emotions of man—for both good and evil. Each believer must, therefore, use this gift wisely. The music we listen to must always be consistent with the character of Christ, whose Name we bear. The songs we sing in church must always present our God and His gospel with accuracy, clarity, and integrity.

The song of praise began at creation, when "the morning stars sang together and all the angels shouted for joy" (Job 38:7). It was restated by the angelic chorus announcing Christ's birth (Luke 2:8-14). It has been proclaimed by the church throughout the centuries. And it is rehearsed each week by worshiping believers everywhere. Furthermore, God's people will continue to sing that song throughout eternity. When we gather for worship and praise, may we pray, "Lord, help me to be a joyful note in the church's endless song."

Group Discussion

1. How would you have answered this boy's question about the purpose of singing in church?
2. What do you feel would be lost if music and singing were eliminated from your church services?
3. If we are not singing, what does this say about our view of life? If this congregation does not sing well, what could this reflect about our church life?
4. In what ways do you feel this saying is true: "A person's practical theology is often his hymnology?"
5. Can you share an experience when a particular song was helpful to you spiritually?
6. What suggestions can you give for improving our praise life both individually and collectively?
7. In what ways can the gift of music be misused in a person's life? In the home? In the church?

Reflections

The voice you are born with is God's gift to you; the use of your voice is your gift to God.   —Unknown

Give me the making of the songs of a nation, and I care not who makes its laws.   —Andrew Fletcher, 1665-1716

Prayer

Lord, I thank You for opportunities to lift my voice in praise and worship of Your Holy Name in this local assembly. Thank you for the refreshment and renewal that singing Your praises brings to our lives. In Christ's Name. AMEN.

O for a Thousand Tongues

CHARLES WESLEY

CARL G. GLÄSER
Mason's *Modern Psalmody*

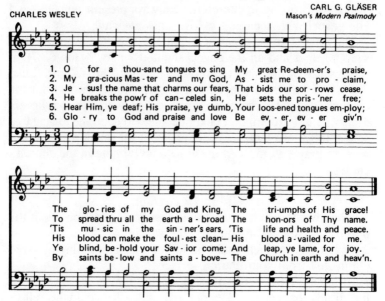

1. O for a thou-sand tongues to sing My great Re-deem-er's praise,
2. My gra-cious Mas-ter and my God, As-sist me to pro-claim,
3. Je-sus! the name that charms our fears, That bids our sor-rows cease,
4. He breaks the pow'r of can-celed sin, He sets the pris-'ner free;
5. Hear Him, ye deaf; His praise, ye dumb, Your loos-ened tongues em-ploy;
6. Glo-ry to God and praise and love Be ev-er, ev-er giv'n

The glo-ries of my God and King, The tri-umphs of His grace!
To spread thru all the earth a-broad The hon-ors of Thy name.
'Tis mu-sic in the sin-ner's ears, 'Tis life and health and peace.
His blood can make the foul-est clean— His blood a-vailed for me.
Ye blind, be-hold your Sav-ior come; And leap, ye lame, for joy.
By saints be-low and saints a-bove— The Church in earth and heav'n.

What Is Christianity?

In the home Christianity is kindness;
In business it is honesty;
In society it is helpfulness;
In work it is fairness;
Toward the unfortunate it is the helping hand;
Toward the weak it is burden bearing;
Toward the strong it is trust;
Toward the sinner it is evangelism;
Toward the erring it is forgiveness;
Toward ourselves it is self-control;
Toward God it is reverence, love and worship. —Unknown

2
THE SONG OF THE CHRISTIAN: PRAISE AND THANKSGIVING

A New Song and Lifestyle
Our Christian Heritage
Our Present Blessings
Our Future Inheritance
Knowing and Doing
Summary
> **Group Discussion**

I will praise God's name in song and will glorify Him with thanksgiving. This will please the Lord...   Psalm 69:30, 31

A New Song and Lifestyle

To become a Christian is to receive a new song for this life and for eternity.

He put a new song in my mouth, a hymn of praise to our God.
—Psalm 40:3

I have told you this so that My joy may be in you and that your joy may be complete.   —John 15:11

This new song expresses our thanksgiving to God and proclaims His holiness.

Many will see and fear and put their trust in the Lord.
—Psalm 40:3

If a man remain in Me and I in him, he will bear much fruit...
—John 15:5

God's people have been called to be *people of praise and thanksgiving.* We are to represent the character of the Almighty—to be living demonstrations to a defiled world of a victorious, joyous lifestyle. A thankful spirit is a mark of Christian maturity.

Our basic attitude toward life is a key factor in our witness and ministry. We make a powerful impression on an unbeliever attending our services when he sees that we are sincerely absorbed in worship and praise. All too often, the non-Christian sees us as a group of apathetic spectators waiting to be entertained.

Praise and thanksgiving could be described as a response of gratitude for the goodness and blessings of God. It's a life that says "thank you" from a redeemed creature for the past, present, and future benefits provided by the Creator. Our praise should include sincere thanksgiving for our Christian heritage, for our daily blessings, and for the anticipation of our eternal inheritance in heaven. We will look at each of these.

Our Christian Heritage

The Scriptures teach that Christians have a great heritage. The foundation for our faith is built upon the apostles and prophets, with Christ Himself the chief cornerstone.

> You are no more strangers and foreigners, but fellow citizens with the saints, and of the household of God; and are built upon the foundation of the apostles and prophets, Jesus Christ Himself being the chief cornerstone.
>
> —Ephesians 2:19, 20, KJV

It can also be stated that the church of Jesus Christ is built on the blood of martyrs. Fox's classic *Book of Martyrs* is filled with examples. Some historians have estimated that at least 50 million persons have had a martyr's death since the crucifixion of Christ. Even today, in our 20th century civilized culture, many thousands around the world suffer and die because of their profession of Christ and witness to His message of love and redemption.

The writer of the Book of Hebrews reminded us that we are "surrounded by a cloud of witnesses" (12:1), including the memory of parents, family, faithful pastors, teachers, and friends who have contributed to our spiritual development. For many of us, a particular individual has especially influenced us. This person has directed us to God, tutored us in truth, and modeled the virtues of Christian life. For me, that person was my father.

Though he had only an eighth grade education, Dad represented God well in his daily living and his local church ministry. As a painter-decorator, he became known to his customers as "the singing painter." Singing his favorite hymns while he worked became his natural way of life. At his funeral, many of his customers told me of the impact my father had upon them as they observed his cheerful attitude while he painted. One of his favorite Sunday afternoon activities was visiting nursing homes, where he would move from one bedside to another with words and songs of cheer. Though the name of Emil Osbeck will never appear in the annals of church history, in my memory he is one of God's choicest saints—and an illustration of the Christian heritage we should cherish.

> For all the saints who from their labors rest,
> Who Thee by faith before the world confessed,
> Thy name, O Jesus, be forever blest.
> Alleluia!   —William W. How

Our Present Blessings

Praise [bless] the Lord, O my soul; all my inmost being, praise His holy name. Praise the Lord, O my soul, and forget not all His benefits.   Psalm 103:1, 2

One important plateau of Christian maturity is learning to enjoy our personal relationship with God and to be content with the life He has given us. Too often believers give the impression that the Christian experience is a cheerless journey of harsh self-discipline that must be painfully endured until the heavenly rewards are finally realized. Little joy or praise is evident in their daily experience.

We ask God to bless and help us. Yet many of our prayers are self-motivated. Scripture teaches that we should bless the Lord and remember His benefits. We need to reflect often on the good things about God listed in the passage:

> Forgives all our iniquities; heals our diseases, redeems our life from destruction; crowns us with loving kindness and mercy; satisfies us with good things; renews our youth, works righteousness and judgment for the oppressed; gives guidance to His people; is merciful; is gracious and slow to anger while plenteous in mercy; knows all about us; will never forsake.
> —Psalm 103:3-10

In the Old Testament, a sacrifice or offering was associated with God's acceptance of man's worship. Christ's entrance into this world was honored by gifts from wisemen: gold, symbolic of His kingly reign; frankincense, symbolic of His priestly ministry; myrrh, symbolic of our redemption through His death. In this New Testament era, believer-priests are also urged to make an appropriate offering — the living, spiritual sacrifice of themselves. *Fundamentally, then, true worship always involves an offering — an attitude of giving rather than getting!*

> I urge you, brothers, in view of God's mercy, to offer your bodies as living sacrifices, holy and pleasing to God—which is your spiritual worship.   —Romans 12:1

Other important spiritual sacrifices desired by God from each believer-priest are:

Praise, Testimony, Good Works, and Sharing

> Through Jesus, therefore, let us continually offer to God a sacrifice of praise—the fruit of lips that confess His name. And do not forget to do good and to share with others, for with such sacrifices God is pleased.   Hebrews 13:15, 16

Have you ever considered your voice as one of the spiritual sacrifices that please God? This gift-offering carries with it a deeply personal reflection of His presence.

As God's people, may we offer the sacrifice of praise continually to the One "who daily loadeth us with benefits" (Psalm 68:19, KJV). May praise and thanksgiving be the antidotes for depression and self-pity. May our times of worship together be pleasing to God because they come from thankful, praising hearts.

> Praise God from whom all blessings flow;
> Praise Him, all creatures here below;
> Praise Him above, ye heav'nly host;
> Praise Father, Son and Holy Ghost.   —Thomas Ken

Our Future Inheritance

Though we are enriched when we reflect on our spiritual heritage and thrilled when we consider the blessings that pour daily into our lives, for the child of God the *best is yet to come:* Heaven! Think of it—an eternity at home with our Lord!

Heaven is not an invention of the human imagination. It is as sure as the promises of God in the Scriptures:

> I am going to prepare a place for you. And if I go and prepare

a place for you, I will come back and take you to be with me
that you also may be where I am.   —John 14:2, 3

As it is written: "No eye has seen, no ear has heard, no mind
has conceived what God has prepared for those who love
Him." But God has revealed it to us by His Spirit.
                                                —1 Corinthians 2:9, 10

In this day of the "throw-away" and the temporary, Christians
must live according to their belief in eternity. The apostle Paul
reminded the believers at Corinth that if their hope in Christ were
related only to this life, they would be the most miserable men
of all (1 Corinthians 15:19). *The anticipation of God's tomorrow
makes it possible for Christians to live joyfully today—regardless
of life's circumstances.* A joyous faith realizes that at best one "sees
through the glass dimly," and that we must accept by faith the
ways of a sovereign God. We look for the day when that imperfect
faith will be rewarded with sight.

Now we see but a poor reflection; then we shall see face to
face. Now I know in part; then I shall know fully, even as I
am fully known.   —1 Corinthians 13:12

What will heaven be like? Golden streets? Jasper walls? Crystal
seas? Jeweled crowns? Certainly—but much, much more! No
mortal mind can comprehend its riches. It is impossible to describe
heavenly scenes with earthly symbols. *One of our major activities
in heaven can be understood, however, because we are preparing
for it now—the worship and praise of our Lord.*

Heaven is revealed to earth as the homeland of music.
                                                —C. Rossetti

When we've been there ten thousand years, bright shining as
the sun; we've no less days to sing God's praise than when we'd
first begun.   —John Newton

Think of stepping on shore, and finding it heaven!
Of taking hold of a hand, and finding it God's hand,
Of breathing new air, and finding it celestial air;
Of feeling invigorated, and finding it immortality,
Of passing from storm and tempest to an unbroken calm,
Of waking up, and finding it Home!   —Unknown

Knowing and Doing

The Lord is my strength and my shield; my heart trusts in Him, and I am helped. My heart leaps for joy and I will give thanks to Him in song.   Psalm 28:7

Most believers agree that the Christian life should be characterized by such words as "joy," "praise," and "thankful." We easily neglect, however, the disciplines and practices that a life of praise and thanksgiving requires.

Our shortcomings can be likened to the response of the ten lepers who were healed by Christ (Luke 17:11-19). Only one returned to express praise and thanks. The life-long remorse of the nine ungrateful lepers is implied in this poem:

I meant to go back, but you may guess
I was filled with amazement I cannot express
To think that after those horrible years,
That terrible loathing and passion of fears,
Of sores unendurable—eaten, defiled—
My flesh was then smooth as the flesh of a child.
I was drunken with joy; I was crazy with glee—
I scarcely could walk and I scarcely could see
For the dazzle of sunshine where all had been black;
But I meant to go back, Oh, I meant to go back!
I had thought to return—then my people came out,
There were tears of rejoicing and laughter and shout;
My cup was so full I seemed nothing to lack—
But I meant to go back; Oh, I meant to go back.
                                                —Anonymous

The following acrostics may help you focus your praise and thanksgiving. Perhaps you can think of other principles and blessings suggested by these letters that will aid in translating such concepts into "thanksliving."

P—Do it *personally.*
R—Do it *repeatedly.*
A—Do it *affectionately.*
I —Do it *intelligently.*
S—Do it *spiritually.*
E—Do it as a preparation for *eternity.*

T—*Treasure,* our income and savings.
H—*Homes,* the places God has given us in which to dwell.
A—*Assurance,* that we are members of God's family.
N—*New Life,* the eternal gift from above.
K—*Kindness,* showered on us by God and His people.
S—*Singing,* as a means of expressing our joy.
G—*Grace,* bestowed liberally and sufficiently.
I —*Intellect,* with which to know and learn about God.
V—*Victory,* over sin by the power of the Spirit.
I —*Insight,* into the truths of God's Word.
N—*Nearness,* God with us in every experience and decision.
G—*Giving,* as a tangible means of thanking Him.

Thanks Giving

I lift my heart to Thee, O God, in gratitude and praise for all Thy blessings of the past, and those of future days—For well I know if I shall live, Thy blessings still shall flow across my soul in greater joy than I could ever know. I thank Thee for my faithful friends, for sunshine and the rain, and every blessing hid or seen, though some may come through pain. O God, accept my thanks to Thee each time I come to pray, and grant each day that I shall live will be THANKS GIVING DAY.

—Unknown

Summary

The mark of a Christian is a life and song of praise and thanksgiving. This is a joyous response to the blessings God has provided for each believer. *Our daily offering to God should be the "sacrifice of praise."*

The joy of the Lord is your strength (Nehemiah 8:10). I will rejoice in the Lord, I will be joyful in God my Savior (Habakkuk 3:18). The fruit of the Spirit is love...against such things there is no law (Galatians 5:22). For the kingdom of God is not a matter of eating and drinking, but of righteousness, peace and *joy in the Holy Spirit,* because anyone who serves Christ in this way is pleasing to God and approved by men (Romans 14:17, 18).

The dedicated Christian is absorbed with God. Praise and thanksgiving ring within and resound from his lips. The pursuit of God's glory, the Lordship of Christ, and the worship and praise of our Creator-redeemer are his natural way of living.

How can I repay the Lord for all His goodness to me? I will lift up the cup of salvation and call on the name of the Lord. I will fulfill my vows to the Lord in the presence of all His people. I will sacrifice a thank offering to You . . . Praise the Lord.   —Psalm 116:12, 13, 14, 17, 19

Group Discussion

1. Tell about someone from your past who influenced your life for God.
2. Reflect on the saying, "What you are speaks so loudly that the world cannot hear what you say." Relate to Matthew 5:16.
3. Share an experience when depression or self-pity was turned into joy through offering God a sacrifice of praise and thanksgiving.
4. If the Christian faith is meant to produce a positive and joyful spirit, why are many believers often perceived as being sad, negative, and burdened by life?
5. What concepts does the word "heaven" bring to your thinking? Relate to 1 John 3:3.
6. What disciplines and practices have you discovered that help you maintain a joyful attitude? What are some major hindrances to a lifestyle of praise and thanksgiving?
7. Is there some definite goal you can pursue this week to bring more praise and thanksgiving into your life? What can we as a congregation do to reflect a greater note of joy in our services?

Reflections

A thankful heart is not only the greatest virtue, but the parent of all the other virtues.   —Cicero

He who sincerely praises God will soon discover within his soul an inclination to praise goodness in his fellow men.

—Unknown

An eternal hope is the oxygen of the human soul.

—Unknown

Saints are persons who make it easier for others to believe in God.

—Unknown

Praise the Savior, Ye Who Know Him

Praise the Savior, ye who know Him!
Who can tell how much we owe Him?
Gladly let us render to Him all we are and have.
Jesus is the name that charms us,
He for conflict fits and arms us;
Nothing moves and nothing harms us while we trust in Him.
Trust in Him, ye saints, forever—He is faithful, changing never;
Neither force nor guile can sever those He loves from Him.
Keep us, Lord,
O keep us cleaving to Thyself, and still believing,
Till the hour of our receiving promised joys with Thee.
Then we shall be where we would be, then we shall be what
    we should be;
Things that are not now, nor could be, soon shall be our own.
—Thomas Kelly, 1769-1854

Prayer

Lord, I thank You for those individuals who have influenced my life for righteousness. May Your daily benefits never become commonplace in my life. Forgive us for becoming so involved in the cares of this life that we lose sight of our heavenly inheritance. May we learn to worship and praise You now in preparation for our occupation throughout eternity. This I pray in Christ's name. AMEN.

3

THE BIBLE AND THE HYMNAL: SOURCES OF OUR SONG

Our Two Books
Understanding the Hymnal's Structure
Appreciating the Hymnal's Contents
Summary
   Group Discussion

Praise the Lord. I will extol the Lord with all my heart in the council
of the upright and in the assembly. . .to Him belongs eternal praise.
                                   Psalm 111:1, 10

Our Two Books

Evangelical Christians have been described as "the people of
the Book." It could accurately be stated, however, that they are
really *the people of two books—the Bible and the hymnal.*

God communicates eternal truth to His people through the
Scriptures. Through the hymnal, we respond to Him with
expressions of worship, praise, and testimony. This two-way
communication, likened to the two wings of a bird, is essential,
if the believer is to experience spiritual maturity and the joy of
Christ. Besides, more is said in the Bible about praise to God
than about any other important activity of worship, including
prayer.

Throughout Protestant history (except for the Bible) the church
hymnal has been the believer's most important book for worship.
Like the Scriptures, however, the hymnal is not always understood
and appreciated.

The purpose of this lesson is to acquaint worshipers with their
church hymnals so that their "sacrifices of praise" might be more
acceptable to God (Hebrews 13:15).

1. Hymnal Category

2. Name of Hymn

HYMNS OF WORSHIP: THE FATHER

4. Author of Words

5. Composer of Music

MARTIN LUTHER, 1483-1546
Trans. by Frederick H. Hedge, 1805-1890

A Mighty Fortress Is Our God

EIN' FESTE BURG

MARTIN LUTHER, 1483-1546

3. Name of Tune

1. A might-y for-tress is our God, A bul-wark nev-er fail - ing;
2. Did we in our own strength con-fide Our striv-ing would be los - ing,
3. And tho this world, with dev-ils filled, Should threaten to un - do us,
4. That word a - bove all earth-ly pow'rs—No thanks to them—a - bid-eth;

Our help-er He a - mid the flood Of mor-tal ills pre - vail - ing.
Were not the right Man on our side, The Man of God's own choos - ing.
We will not fear, for God hath willed His truth to tri-umph thru us.
The Spir-it and the gifts are ours Thru Him who with us sid - eth.

For still our an-cient foe Doth seek to work us woe— His craft and
Dost ask who that may be? Christ Je-sus, it is He— Lord Sab - a -
The prince of dark-ness grim— We trem-ble not for him; His rage we
Let goods and kin-dred go, This mor-tal life al - so; The bod-y

pow'r are great, And, armed with cru-el hate, On earth is not his e - qual.
oth His name, From age to age the same— And He must win the bat - tle.
can en - dure, For lo! his doom is sure— One lit-tle word shall fell him.
they may kill: God's truth a - bid-eth still— His king-dom is for - ev - er.

6. Ownership of Hymn

Understanding the Hymnal's Structure

Using the first important hymn written during the 16th century Protestant Reformation, "A Mighty Fortress Is Our God," we will identify and explain the structural information and indexes found in most church hymnals.

1. *The Hymn Categories*

Each hymn is given a subject classification by the editors of the hymnal. Hymns of the same type are usually grouped together. A table of contents located at the front of the hymnal shows the broad organization of the book. Examples might be:

Hymns of Worship
God the Father
Jesus Our Savior
The Holy Spirit
The Word of God
The Church
The Christian Experience

God's Love for Us
Our Love for God
Our Love for the
  Family of God
Our Love for Others

These general classfications are usually subdivided into smaller categories in the Topical Index listings, usually found at the back of the book. The editors classify each hymn by detailed subject. For example, "A Mighty Fortress Is Our God" might be found under these topics:

Assurance, Christian Warfare, Church, God our Father, Providence, Security, Victory, Worship.

2. *The Name of the Hymn*

Following the Topical Index is usually the General Index, which lists the hymn titles alphabetically in small caps. The first lines of the hymns, because they are familiar, are given in lower case type.

3. *The Name of the Tune*

The tune for our sample hymn is called "Ein' Feste Burg." In the early days of hymn publishing, tune names were very important. This is because the words only were printed in a hymnal. Leaders of a service would announce both the hymn text to be sung and the particular tune to be used. Many of these tune names have an interesting history. Some were named after the person who composed the melody, while others stated the place where the text or tune were written. Still others were dedicated to certain individuals or churches and some others were given distinctive names by a hymnal editorial committee.

Metrical Index

The Metrical Index is closely related to the tune names and is generally placed at the back of the book. This index shows the metrical forms for the hymns. The number of digits shown indicates the number of lines per stanza, while each digit indicates the number of syllables receiving an accent in each line of poetry. "A Mighty Fortress Is Our God" has a metrical form of 87.87.66.667

		1	2	3	4	5	6	7	8
Line 1	A	might-	y	for -	tress	is	our	God	
		1	2	3	4	5	6	7	
Line 2	A	bul -	wark	nev	- er	fail	- ing;		
		1	2	3	4	5	6	7	8
Line 3	Our	help	- er	He	a -	mid	the	flood	
		1	2	3	4	5	6	7	
Line 4	Of	mor -	tal	ills	pre -	vail	- ing.		
		1	2	3	4	5	6		
Line 5	For	still	our	an -	cient	foe			
		1	2	3	4	5	6		
Line 6	Doth	seek	to	work	us	woe—			
		1	2	3	4	5	6		
Line 7	His	craft	and	pow'r	are	great,			
		1	2	3	4	5	6		
Line 8	And,	armed	with	cru	- el	hate,			
		1	2	3	4	5	6	7	
Line 9	On	earth	is	not	His	e -	qual.		

The following meters are the most widely used:

Number of Lines	Meter Names	Number of Syllables for each line
Four	Short Meter (SM)	6.6.8.6.—Usually used for texts that are emphatic and tense. "I Love Thy Kingdom, Lord"
Four	Common Meter (CM)	8.6.8.6.—Provides more flexibility to a text. "Amazing Grace"
Four	Long Meter (LM)	8.8.8.8.—Used for texts that are more stately and dignified. "Jesus Shall Reign"
Four	10's	10.10.10.10.
Six	Long Perfect Meter (LPM)	8.8.8.8.8.8.

When a D is added (L.M.D., C.M.D., S.M.D.), it indicates that the entire pattern has been doubled. When the pattern differs from any of the above structures, the meter is indicated with Arabic numerals. Example—8.7.8.7; 10.10.10.11.11.11. Other meter designations used are:

With Refrain: Indicates that an additional phrase or short portion is to be sung after each verse.

With Alleluias: Indicates that the verses of the hymn include an "alleluia." Example—"Christ the Lord Is Risen Today." 7.7.7.7. with Alleluias.

Irregular: Indicates that the lines of the different verses do not always contain the same number of syllables.

The Metrical Index lists the various meters with hymn tune names shown below them. Thus, one tune may serve as music for several hymn texts. The leader of congregational singing may use the Metrical Index to interchange the tunes for hymns that share the same meter. For example, a Common Meter tune (8.6.8.6.) such as "Amazing Grace" could be sung with the "Arlington" tune used for the hymn, "Am I a Soldier of the Cross?" The use of a different tune may make the words of a familiar hymn fresh again.

4. *The Author of the Words (Text)*

The author's name appears at the upper left side of the page. As you can see, "A Mighty Fortress Is Our God" was written by Martin Luther (1483-1546). The index section of many hymnals has a listing called the "Index of Authors, Composers, and Sources" including translators and arrangers. This is an alphabetical listing of the people who wrote the words and composed the music for each hymn. The dates of the birth and death of each writer are designated. If the hymn was orginally written in a language other than English, the translator and source are shown. In the case of Luther's hymn, Frederick H. Hedge translated the hymn from German to English in the 19th century.

5. *The Composer of the Music*

This information is given at the upper right side of the page. For our sample hymn, the tune is also credited to Martin Luther. As mentioned above, both the author of text and the composers of the music are listed in an "Index of Composers, Arrangers, and Sources." The Index also gives the sources of the original tunes. Many of our hymn melodies have been borrowed from older songs, folk tunes, or carols from other lands.

6. *The Owner of the Hymn*

A copyright is a legal protection for the person or company owning the hymn. The copyright law insures that no one can publish, reproduce, arrange, or record a hymn without the owner's permission. This protection was first provided by the United States Copyright Act of 1831 and later by the Copyright Act of 1909 as amended. Under the 1909 law, a copyrighted hymn was protected for 28 years. Before the expiration of that period, the owner could apply for a 28 year extension. After 56 years, the hymn became "public domain," meaning that anyone was free to use and publish it.

A new copyright law became effective on January 1, 1978. Under this law, a copyright renewed after the initial 28 year period can be extended for an additional 47 years. Total copyright protection is now 75 years. Under the provisions of this new law, hymns written and copyrighted after January 1, 1978 will be protected for the life of the author, plus 50 years.

If the copyright is still in effect, the information will be shown at the bottom of the page. For "A Mighty Fortress Is Our God," the copyright expired long ago. It is in public domain.

Devotional Materials

In addition to the above indexes, many church hymnals also provide a number of excellent worship and devotional resources. These include suggested Scripture readings and other inspirational works. Because of this, a hymnal is an excellent tool for personal and family devotions.

Appreciating the Hymnal's Contents

The study of hymns can be a rewarding experience. Some have spoken of this study as the "romance of sacred song." To realize how Christians through the centuries have responded to God, to share in the spiritual expressions of others, and to comprehend the emotional and physical struggles that caused our hymns to be written are thrilling discoveries.

Here is a suggestion. The next time you open your hymnal, think about the words you are singing. Make an effort to learn the background of your favorite hymns. Take time to enjoy informal sessions of singing hymns with family and friends. The church hymnal can be a significant tool in every Christian's life—in church services, in the Christian education of children, and in family and personal devotions. Let us grow in appreciation and use of the hymnal, the second most important book in the believer's worship and praise.

Summary

Evangelical churches and individual Christians should become familiar with and use both of their basic books for worshiping God—the Bible and the hymnal. The Bible is God's self-disclosure to man. It spells out God's plan of redemption. It is our final authority for all matters of faith, morals, and practice. Through the inspired Word, God the Holy Spirit illuminates and guides the believer in his Christian walk.

All Scripture is God-breathed and is useful for teaching, rebuking, correcting and training in righteousness, so that the man of God may be thoroughly equipped for every good work.
—2 Timothy 3:16, 17

Thy Word Is Like A Garden, Lord

Thy Word is like a garden, Lord, with flowers bright and fair;
And ev'ry one who seeks may pluck a lovely cluster there.
Thy Word is like a deep, deep mine, and jewels rich and rare
Are hidden in its mighty depths for ev'ry searcher there.

Thy Word is like a starry host—A thousand rays of light
Are seen to guide the traveler, and make his pathway bright.
Thy Word is like an armory where soldiers may repair
And find, for life's long battle day, all needful weapons there.

O may I love Thy precious Word, may I explore the mine;
May I its fragrant flowers glean, may light upon me shine.
O may I find my armor there, Thy Word my trusty sword!
I'll learn to fight with ev'ry foe the battle of the Lord!
—Edwin Hodder

Congregational praise through song is an important part of worship and witness. The church hymnal, a collection of man's noblest responses to God, is vital not only for our worship services, but also for our individual spiritual growth and devotional use.

But you are a chosen people, a royal priesthood, a holy nation, a people belonging to God, *that you may declare the praises of Him* who called you out of darkness into His wonderful light.
—1 Peter 2:9

Hymns breathe the praise of the saints, the vision of the prophets, the prayers of the penitent, and the spirit of the martyrs. They bring solace to the sad, assurance to the perplexed, faith to the doubter, and comfort to the oppressed. They span the centuries of history and cross the barriers of denominations. Study them to be pure in heart; sing them to be joyful in spirit. Store them in the mind to possess a treasury of worship.

Group Discussion

1. Leaf through and discuss your church hymnal together. Note its structure, the various categories of hymns, the authors, the composers, and the various indexes—general, topical, tune, and metrical. Investigate the worship and devotional resources and readings. Encourage the congregation to use the entire hymnal.
2. List the group's ten favorite hymns. Tell why these hymns have been especially meaningful. If possible, give the background of some of the hymns.*
3. Try singing different tunes with hymns that have the same meter. What is your reaction to this practice?
4. What do you feel are the purposes of a song service?
5. What do you most enjoy about congregational singing? What activities are most distracting or annoying in a song service?
6. Give constructive suggestions for improving the congregational singing in your church.
7. Make an effort this week to use your church hymnal as part of your personal or family devotions. Be ready to share your experience.

Reflections

More is said in the Bible about praise than prayer. Music and song have not only accompanied all Scriptural revivals, but are essential in deepening one's spiritual life. Singing does at least as much as preaching to impress the Word of God upon people's minds. Ever since God first called me, the importance of praise expressed in song has grown upon me.   —D.L. Moody
Living a life without prayer and praise is like building a house without nails.   —Unknown

---

* *101 Hymn Stories* and *101 More Hymn Stories* by Kenneth W. Osbeck, Grand Rapids: Kregel Publications, 1983, 1984.

Sing Unto The Lord

He listened as the pastor spoke,
And bowed his head for prayer;
And when the off'ring plate was passed
He gladly gave his share.

But when a hymn was wont to sing
He tightly sealed his tongue,
Till songs of praise that cried for strength
Were weak and feebly sung.

Not just because he failed to sing,
But others joined him, too,
And mocked with hollow silence
The praises of the few.

Forgive us, Lord, who fail to see
The glory of the song,
That nobly lifts the name of Christ
Above all sin and wrong.

And tune our hearts to sing Thy praise
Until each sincere soul
Shall stand condemned within his heart
To shrink back from our goal—

The goal that each heart born anew
May gladly join our song;
Not just within the worship hour,
But through the whole day long.

—Ronald K. Wells

Prayer

O God of Eternal beauty and harmony, Who has ordained that men shall declare Your glory in the joy of music, anoint with Your Spirit all who, by voice or instrument, lead the praises of Your people, that in sincerity and truth, we may ever magnify Your name in concert with saints and angels. This is our prayer in Christ's holy name. AMEN.

4

THE SONG OF ISRAEL:
THE OLD TESTAMENT

David told the leaders of the Levites to appoint their brothers as singers to sing joyful songs, accompanied by musical instruments: lyres, harps, and cymbals.   1 Chronicles 15:16

Search the Scriptures

When Christians wish to learn about a new topic, they should first "search the Scriptures" (Acts 17:11). Opening our minds to God's Word lets the Holy Spirit enlighten our understanding and helps us to think God's thoughts.

Our next two lessons will be an examination of the biblical teaching about music and worship in both the Old and New Testaments. From the Old Testament we will discover that music was an important and integral part of Jewish life. We will learn about the musicians, choirs, and musical instruments used in Jewish worship, requirements for the music leaders, and the way music was used. We will also learn that God refused to hear the songs of His people on occasion because their public praise was inconsistent with their daily living.

The Old Testament has much to teach us about music and worship. It has valuable lessons that can be applied to church music ministries today.

Music and the Old Testament

But Thou art holy, O Thou who inhabitest the praises of Israel.
Psalm 22:3 (KJV)

The pages of the Old Testament are alive with the sounds of music. In fact, song and Jewish history are almost synonymous. From the joyous chants of the Exodus onward, the religious feelings of the Jewish faithful were made known in song and dance. No person contributed more to the role of music in Jewish life than King David, who has been called the "sweet singer of Israel." The Hebrews probably derived many of the musical practices and instruments from their neighbors—the Egyptians, Babylonians, and Assyrians. In marked contrast to the contemporary religions of that day, however, the Israelites were known for their use of music in the worship of the one true God, Jehovah.

The joy of Jewish song was stilled during the Babylonian exile. One of their songs, Psalm 137, records their sad lament during that period:

By the rivers of Babylon we sat and wept when we remembered Zion. There on the poplars we hung our harps, for there our captors asked us for songs, our tormentors demanded songs of joy; they said "Sing us one of the songs of Zion!" How can we sing the songs of the Lord in a foreign land? (vv. 1-4)

When the Jews returned to Jerusalem to rebuild the temple, joyful singing returned. In fact, music was always an indication of Israel's spiritual relationship with God. The sound of music was frequently associated with an awareness of God's presence. Whenever music was absent from the service of Jehovah, the nation was going through a period of judgment and spiritual desolation.

Music — A Way Of Life

Music was an important part of Old Testament life. It was the natural expression of Israelite feelings on nearly every occasion, secular and religious.

Religious: The worship by Israel was richly expressed in music (1 Chronicles 15:14, 27, 28; 16:4-7, 23-30; 25:1-31; 2 Chronicles 30:21; Nehemiah 12:45-47).

Social: Social occasions such as weddings were made more enjoyable through music (1 Samuel 1:18-27).

Funerals: Music was used for mourning as well as for times of gladness. Note the dirge (funeral song) sung by David with the deaths of Saul and Jonathan (2 Samuel 1:18-27).

Economic: Important times of prosperity for the Jews, such as grape gatherings and grain harvests, were celebrated with music (Isaiah 16:10; 27:2; Jeremiah 48:33).

Political: When a king was crowned, great performances of music helped people celebrate the coronations (2 Kings 1:39-40; 2 Kings 9:13; 11:14; 2 Chronicles 23:11-13). When military victories were celebrated, the people expressed their joy with voices and instruments (Exodus 15:1-21; Judges 5:1-31; 11:34; 1 Samuel 18:6, 7; 2 Chronicles 20:21, 22, 27, 28).

Individual Musicans

One of the first musicians mentioned in the Old Testament was Moses. He led the people of Israel in singing of God's power in their deliverance from the Egyptians (Exodus 15). Miriam, his sister, joined in this songfest as a soloist (vv. 20, 21). Deborah and Barak lifted glad voices in praise to God for their miraculous victory over the Canaanites (Judges 5:1, 2). Asaph led a group of instrumentalists and singers when the ark was brought to Jerusalem (1 Chronicles 15 and 16). Other musicians mentioned in the Old Testament include Jeduthum (1 Chronicles 16:38, 42); Chenaniah (1 Chronicles 15:27); Jezrahiah (Nehemiah 12:42), and Habakkuk (Habakkuk 3:19).

Organized Choirs

The Old Testament records several organized choirs. One of them was David's tabernacle choir, composed of ten men and a director (1 Chronicles 15:12-22; 16:4, 5). King Solomon organized a 4,000 voice choir for the dedication of the temple. Its awe-inspiring performance was accompanied by a large body of musical instruments, and it filled the new temple with the glory of God (1 Chronicles 23:5; 27-32; 2 Chronicles 5:11-14). Zerubbabel's temple choir was composed of 200 mixed voices (Ezra 2:41, 65, 70; 3:10-13; 24:10-24). Nehemiah's choir had 245 voices (Nehemiah 7:1; 11:22, 23; 12:27-30; 13:5, 10).

The first-century Jewish historian, Josephus, stated that as many as 200,000 persons had been trained for the musical portions of the temple service.*

Musical Instruments

The musical instruments mentioned in the Old Testament were used to accompany singing, especially in the temple worship. These instruments can be divided into three groups: strings, wind, and percussion. We will look at each.

Strings:
   Harp or Kinnor. Thought to be like a portable lyre with ten strings (1 Samuel 10:5; 26:23; 1 Kings 10:12).
   Psaltery or Nebel. Thought to be a lute-like instrument with a bulging, resonant body at its lower end. It was played by plucking the strings with the fingers rather than with a plectrum (Daniel 3:5).
   Sackbut. This is a stringed instrument mentioned in Daniel 3, that was part of Nebuchadnezzar's orchestra. Some translations treat the Sackbut as a wind instrument, a kind of brass trumpet with a slide. Most scholars feel, however, that it was a small triangular harp of four or more strings with high pitch.
   Dulcimer. This orchestral instrument mentioned in Daniel 3 is thought to have been some form of bagpipe.
Wind Instruments:
   Pipe. Probably an early predecessor of the oboe and clarinet. It seems to have been used especially for festival processions (Isaiah 30:29), or at times of national rejoicing (1 Kings 1:40).
   Flute. This orchestral instrument, also mentioned in Daniel 3, was a high-sounding instrument that whistled or hissed.
   Organ. This term was used for all wind instruments.
   Horns, trumpets (or shofars), and cornets. The earliest of these instruments were made out of the horns of animals. Later they were imitated in metal. The shofar (ram's horn) is still used in Jewish services.

---

*Flavius Josephus. *The Complete Works of Josephus.* Grand Rapids: Kregel Publications, 1960.

Percussion:
Bells. These instruments produced sound when struck.
Cymbals. Always mentioned in connection with religious ceremonies. There were evidently two kinds of cymbals. One kind had two shallow metal plates, one held in each hand and struck together. The others were cup-like in shape, one held stationary while the other was brought down sharply against it.
Timbrels and Tabrets. A tambourine-type instrument that was played by holding and striking with the hand. It is always associated with joy and gladness (Isaiah 5:12; 1 Samuel 18:6). (Interestingly, there is no mention of the use of drums in the Old Testament.)

Requirements of Music Leaders

The Levites were the appointed worship-music leaders of the Old Testament. They performed an important and sacred function in Israelite worship. The Levites had to meet strict requirements because they were in the service of a holy God. Consider these ten requirements recorded in the Old Testament for music leaders:

1. They were chosen from the levitical priesthood—not just anyone could serve in this capacity (1 Chronicles 15:1, 2; 11-22; 16:4-7; 37:41, 42; 2 Chronicles 20:21; Nehemiah 7:1).
2. They were well organized—they were assigned specific work and were individually appointed to their tasks (2 Chronicles 7:6; 8:14; 29:25; 31:2; Nehemiah 11:2).
3. They were educated and trained—teachers as well as scholars (1 Chronicles 15:22; 25:1-8; Nehemiah 11:22; 12:42, 46).
4. They were efficient performers—punctual and systematic. The word "skillful" is often used of them (1 Chronicles 16:37; 2 Chronicles 8:14; 15:22; 31:2).
5. They were consecrated; that is, they had clean hands and pure hearts (Numbers 8:5-16; 1 Chronicles 15:12, 14, 16; 2 Chronicles 5:11, 12).
6. They were models of obedience to God's Word (2 Chronicles 34:30-32).
7. They were set apart by wearing distinctive robes (1 Chronicles 15:27; 2 Chronicles 5:12).
8. They were paid for their services (Numbers 18:21; 2 Chronicles 31:2-10; Nehemiah 12:57; 13:5, 10, 11). Homes were provided for them (Ezra 2:70; Nehemiah 7:73; 12:28, 29).

9. They were treated as other religious leaders, with no discrimination (Ezra 7:24; Nehemiah 10:28, 29, 39).

10. They were to be mature (only those age 30 and over). The worship of God was not to be performed by the young and inexperienced (Numbers 4:47; 1 Chronicles 23:3-5).

To minister musically in Old Testament days was both a great privilege and a solemn responsibility. It required special people who were well prepared. This should still be true of the music ministry in the church today. In some senses, those who minister musically now are New Testament Levites. Therefore, the principles established by God for the levitical priesthood can be used as valid guidelines for music leaders in a New Testament church.

Practices and Procedures

A special school was established in Solomon's day for training musicians. We are told that 288 people taught the singers in the temple choir (1 Chronicles 25:7, 8). The musicians were referred to as "seers," implying that they had special spiritual insights (1 Chronicles 25:5; 2 Chronicles 29:30; 35:15). Since music notation was not developed at this time, the music was memorized and sung in unison with instrumental accompaniment. The melodies were thought to be chant-like, in a limited range. They were sung with much embellishment. The "selahs" are thought to have been instrumental interludes, giving the singers and worshipers opportunity to reflect on what had just been sung. The directors used a system of hand signs known as "chaironomy" when leading the musicians. The music was probably based on the Pentatonic Scale, a five note scale much like our present black keys on the piano.

The temple service was an inspiring, active, and dramatic spectacle. As the people worshiped, they responded physically. Note these Bible references that suggest physical involvement:

1. They shouted for joy (Psalm 32:11; 35:27; 47:1; 132:9, 16).
2. They sang with loud voices (Psalm 33:3; 81:1; 98:4).
3. They used their lips (Psalm 63:3, 5; 119:171).
4. They made solemn sounds (Psalm 92:3).
5. They stood (1 Chronicles 23:30; Nehemiah 9:5).
6. They clapped their hands (Psalm 47:1).
7. They raised their hands (Psalm 28:2, 119:48; 134:2).

8. They danced (Psalm 149:3; 150:4).
9. They bowed and knelt (Psalm 95:6).
10. They were quiet (Psalm 46:10).

Antiphonal singing was widely practiced in temple worship. Different choirs and groups of instruments answered each other, or the choir answered the leader. This was possible because Hebrew poetry used parallel couplets to form a series of balanced phrases. For example, look at Psalm 24:

a. The earth is the Lord's, and everything in it,
b. The world, and all who live in it.
a. For He founded it upon the seas,
b. And established it upon the water.
a. Who may ascend the hill of the Lord?
b. Who may stand in His holy place?

Synagogue Worship

After the Jewish dispersions, worship centered in the Synagogue. The Scriptures were discussed, the leaders chanted prayers, and the congregation sang songs and canticles. Temple choirs were replaced by leaders known as cantors, soloists trained in the traditions of the Levitical temple service.

Musical Sounds That Displease God

Though music had an exalted place in Israel's worship and praise of Jehovah, the Scriptures teach that at times their music was not acceptable to God. Public worship and praise must always be consistent with personal righteousness and social justice. *The music of the church must be lived as well as performed.* Without personal holiness, public praise becomes an abomination to the Lord — songs that He refuses to hear! Consider these passages:

Even though you bring Me burnt offerings and grain offerings, I will not accept them. Though you bring choice fellowship offerings, I will have no regard for them. Away with the noise of your songs! I will not listen to the music of your harps. But let justice roll on like a river, righteousness like a never-failing stream.   —Amos 5:21-24

Woe to you who are complacent in Zion. . .you lie on beds inlaid with ivory and lounge on your couches. You dine on choice lambs and fattened calves. You strum away on your harps

like David and improvise on musical instruments. You drink
wine by the bowlful and use the finest lotions, but you do not
grieve over the ruin of Joseph. —Amos 6:1a, 4-6

Summary
The New Testament teaches that the Old Testament is important
for our learning and encouragement. Consider these verses:

These things happened to them as an example and they were
written for our instruction... —1 Corinithans 10:11

For everything that was written in the past was written to teach
us, so that through endurance and the encouragement of the
Scriptures we might have hope. —Romans 15:4

From a study of the Old Testament we are impressed with the
truth that God desires worship from His people, expressed with
voices and instruments of praise. "Let everything that has breath
praise the Lord" (Psalm 150:6).

The Old Testament Jews are models to us, for they were people
with a great song. God used the Levites, who were both dedicated
and qualified, to lead His people in worship. The warning is clear,
however, that the songs of praise from God's people must be
consistent with their hearts and their lives. If not, the worship
is not acceptable to Him.

May these words of consecration reflect our desire as we worship
the eternal God:

Take my life and let it be consecrated, Lord, to Thee;
Take my voice and let me sing always, only, for my King.
Take my love — my God, I pour at Thy feet its treasure store;
Take myself — and I will be ever, only, all for Thee.
—Frances Ridley Havergal

Group Discussion
1. It is important to sing in a church service. Why is it even more
important for a Christian to carry a song into his daily life?
2. Do we place as much importance on music in church worship
today as did the Israelites in the Old Testament temple? Why?
3. In what ways do the requirements for levitical leadership in
the Old Testament apply to the music leaders in the local church
today?

4. Do you feel that music directors, accompanists, soloists, groups, and individual choir members should be paid for their services? Why?

5. Should persons with excellent voices or instrumental talents be permitted to minister musically in a church service when their Christian testimony is questionable?

6. To what degree should we be physically involved in worship?

7. What practical lessons from the Old Testament about music and worship could enhance the ministry of this church?

Reflections

Christianity is not a theory or speculation, but a life; not a philosophy of life, but a living presence. This realization can turn any gloom into a song.   —Samuel Taylor Coleridge

Happiness is not perfected until it is shared.   —Unknown

The God of Abraham Praise!

The God of Abraham praise, who reigns enthroned above,
Ancient of everlasting days, and God of love.
Jehovah, great I AM, by earth and heav'n confessed,
I bow and bless the sacred name forever blest.

The God who reigns on high the great archangels sing,
And "Holy, holy, holy" cry, "Almighty King!"
Who was and is the same, and evermore shall be:
Jehovah, Father, great I AM, we worship Thee.

The whole triumphant host give thanks to God on high;
"Hail, Father, Son and Holy Ghost!" They ever cry.
Hail, Abraham's God and mine! I join the heav'nly lays;
All might and majesty are Thine, and endless praise.

A synagogue melody based on the Jewish Doxology
—Thomas Olivers

Prayer

Dear Lord, help me carry the song of the Lord into my life. May I be filled with Your joy, as Your people were in Old Testament times. Show me when my witness is weakened by negative attitudes. And let the music ministry of our church challenge each believer with the goal of victorious, joyful living, that together we will glorify You. This we pray in our Savior's name. AMEN.

5
THE SONG OF THE EARLY CHURCH: THE NEW TESTAMENT

Who shall separate us from the love of Christ? Shall trouble or hardship or persecution or famine or nakedness or danger or sword? No, in all these things we are more than conquerors through Him who loved us. Romans 8:35, 37

Music and the New Testament

Though music had an exalted place in the temple worship of the Old Testament, the congregation was not completely involved. The professional leaders, the Levitical priests, offered the animal sacrifices to God on behalf of the people. But in the New Testament church, where each Christian is positionally a priest before God, everyone attending the service is a participant. Believers are instructed to offer their bodies as sacrifices (Romans 12:1). And they are to present spiritual sacrifices of praise directly to God through the use of psalms, hymns, and songs (Hebrews 13:15; Ephesians 5:19; Colossians 3:16).

Early Christian Worship

For a brief time, Christians of the first century met for worship in the synagogues. But they preferred to have their "love-feasts" and communion services in their own homes (Acts 2:46). Chanting and antiphonal psalm-singing very likely became part of the worship of these early believers.

For the first few centuries, the church suffered through several periods of severe persecution by the Roman Empire. This forced the believers to assemble secretly in homes, and even to hide in catacombs. Here are key dates, events, and people who influenced the early church.

A. D. c. 33   Pentecost. The first New Testament church.

54-68   Emperor Nero's reign. The first serious persecution of the early Christians outside Palestine.

c. 56   The apostle Paul's letter to the church at Rome. Read Romans 8:28-39 in light of the persecution being suffered by these believers.

70   The destruction of the temple in Jerusalem.

135   Jerusalem destroyed and the Jews dispersed throughout the Roman Empire.

313   Christianity legalized through the Roman Empire during the reign of Constantine 1, who ruled from 306-337. This era is known as "the peace of the church."

330   The dedication of the new eastern capital of the Roman Empire in Constantinople (now Istanbul). This resulted in the spread of the Byzantine influence throughout Christendom.

381   Christianity declared to be the official religion of the Roman State. The beginning of the phenomenal growth of the church.

354-430   Augustine. Next to Paul, Augustine is considered the most influential early church leader. His writings, "Confessions" and "The City of God," were important in defining and establishing church doctrine.

340-391   St. Ambrose, Bishop of Milan. He encouraged congregational singing and combatted doctrinal error by teaching spiritual truths through hymn singing. However, a church council soon decreed: "If laymen are not to interpret the Scriptures for themselves, so they are not to sing the songs of the church."

455 Rome destroyed by vandals. The decline of the
Roman Empire.

540-604 Pope Gregory. An important developer and
organizer of the church's music. Gregorian chants
became the basis of Catholic church music and
the church's liturgy, the Mass. These chants have
since been regarded by many musicians as the
supreme model for sacred music. (The hymn tune,
"When I Survey the Wondrous Cross," is said to
have been a Gregorian chant).

All music in the early church was vocal, because instrumental
music was associated with boisterous Roman paganism. The words
were considered most important, not the music. This music (called
monody) is described by such terms as "plain song," "plain chant,"
and "Gregorian chant." These chants were borrowed from Hebrew
temple and synagogue services, and they consisted mainly of the
intoned reciting of the psalms. Biblical texts used that were not
psalms were called "canticles." The music of the early church,
moreover, increasingly became the music of the clergy. This led
to the development of music as an art form in the Catholic church.
*It ruled out, however, lay participation in congregational
singing—the church's true song.*

New Testament references to music are limited. The most direct
teaching about the practice of church music is found in Paul's
letters to the churches at Ephesus and Colosse (Ephesians 5:19;
Colossians 3:16). These passages teach that the early New
Testament believers, despite their hardships and persecutions, were
to continue to sing during their worship with the use of psalms,
hymns and spiritual songs. The book of Revelation closes the New
Testament record by vibrating with a great, eternal psalm of praise
to the sovereign Creator, Redeemer, and Lord.

Psalms

Do not get drunk on wine, which leads to debauchery. Instead be
filled with the Spirit. Speak to one another with *psalms*, hymns and
spiritual songs. Sing and make music in your heart to the Lord, always
giving thanks to God the Father for everything, in the name of our
Lord Jesus Christ.   Ephesians 5:18-20

This passage teaches us several important truths:

1. A joy-filled life is directly related to our being "filled with
the Spirit."

2. New Testament believers were to interact with one another. They were to take an active part in giving praise and thanks to God in the name of their Savior.

3. Our psalms, hymns and spiritual songs should minister to us spiritually. We are to use these musical forms in ministering to others (Colossians 3:16). Church music, then, must always be thought of as a ministry, not as entertainment (James 5:13).

4. Our musical expressions are to be directed "to the Lord." Musicians should be focused on God as they play and sing.

5. Our songs should produce joy. It has been said that if there were more singing Christians, there would be more Christians.

6. A church's music ministry should be marked by a balance of musical styles as represented by "psalms, hymns, and spiritual songs."

The psalms were in use at the feast in the temple in which the disciples and Jesus participated, including the Passover (John 2:13), and the Feast of Tabernacles (John 7:2-9). Most likely, some first-century believers questioned whether the Old Testament songs, the psalms, were still appropriate for New Testament worship. The word "psalm" literally means "a song of praise." It implies more than just the 150 psalms, but rather any of the exalted expressions of praise found throughout the Old Testament.

In Ephesians 5:19, Paul made it clear that New Testament Christians were not to neglect this important part of their heritage. They needed the lofty expressions of God's majesty and power that appear in the psalms and other Old Testament Scriptures. Without these reminders from the past, believers tend to limit God to their present experience and understanding. Every generation needs to hear the psalmist's perspective of God and his views of man and eternity—that God is eternal and worthy of man's worship, praise, and service (Psalm 90:1, 2). The psalms are the true classics of church music. Therefore, with Apostle Paul we echo, *DON'T NEGLECT THE SINGING OF THE PSALMS!*

Hymns

Let the word of Christ dwell in you richly as you teach and admonish one another with all wisdom, and as you sing psalms, *hymns* and spiritual songs with gratitude in your hearts to God.Colossians 3:16

This verse suggests five characteristics of church music:

1. The more prominence a Christian gives the Scriptures, the more joyful his life will be.
2. We are to use music to instruct and encourage one another.
3. Our singing should employ a balance of musical styles—psalms, hymns, and spiritual songs.
4. Our singing must be based upon our personal experience of God's grace.
5. Singers must always direct their songs "to the Lord."

For first-century Christians, hymns were newer religious expressions that extolled the works and teachings of Christ. They taught New Testament doctrine and they applied the Christian faith to life. Many Bible scholars feel that the following passages were actually hymns sung by the early church: Ephesians 5:14; Philippians 2:5-11; 1 Timothy 3:16; 2 Timothy 2:11-13; Titus 3:14; Revelation 4:11.

The oldest hymn text with a known author is "Shepherd of Eager Youth." This hymn still appears in many hymnals today.

Shepherd of Eager Youth

ITALIAN HYMN

Clement of Alexandria, c. 170-c.220
Trans. by Henry Martyn Dexter, 1821-1890

Felice De Giardini, 1716-1796

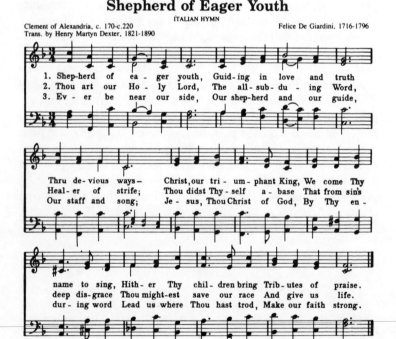

1. Shep-herd of ea - ger youth, Guid-ing in love and truth
2. Thou art our Ho - ly Lord, The all - sub-du - ing Word,
3. Ev - er be near our side, Our shep-herd and our guide,

Thru de-vious ways— Christ, our tri - um - phant King, We come Thy
Heal-er of strife; Thou didst Thy-self a - base That from sin's
Our staff and song; Je - sus, Thou Christ of God, By Thy en-

name to sing, Hith - er Thy chil - dren bring Trib - utes of praise.
deep dis-grace Thou might-est save our race And give us life.
dur - ing word Lead us where Thou hast trod, Make our faith strong.

Clement of Alexandria wrote the hymn text in the Greek language between A.D. 202 and the time of this death in 220. The Greek title of this hymn could literally be translated "Tamer of Steeds Unbridled." It was used as a hymn of Christian instruction for young people converted from paganism. Clement felt it was the church's responsibility to tame the wills of the youth, and to train them in doctrine so they would be profitable servants of Christ.

Defining Hymns

Hymns may be defined as poetic expressions of praise, adoration, worship, confession, and vows of service addressed to God. The music and the words are marked with a sense of lofty reverence, yet with enough simplicity to be sung by an assembly of people. The texts are essentially God-centered in character.

In the fourth century, Augustine described a hymn as follows:

Do you know what a hymn is? It is singing to the praise of God. If you praise God and do not sing, you utter no hymn. If you sing and praise not God, you utter no hymn. If you praise anything which does not pertain to the praise of God, though in singing you praise, you utter no hymn.

The Hymn Society of America gives this definition:

A Christian hymn is a lyric poem, reverently and devotionally conceived, which is designed to be sung and which expresses the worshiper's attitude toward God or God's purposes in human life. It should be simple and metrical in form, genuinely emotional, poetic and literary in style, spiritual in quality, and in its ideas so direct and so immediately apparent as to unify a congregation while singing it.

The Power of a Hymn

There's something about a fine old hymn
That can stir the heart of a man;
That can reach to the goal of his inmost soul
Such as no mere preaching can.
It's more than the tune of the song he sings
And it's more than the poet's rhyme;
It's the Spirit of God working through these things
That gives them their power sublime!

So we thank Thee, Lord, for the fine old hymns;
May we use them again and again;
As we seek to save from a hopeless grave
The souls of our fellow men.

—Author Unknown

Since the hymn is the foundation of the church's music, with the apostle Paul we echo, *DON'T NEGLECT THE SINGING OF HYMNS!*

Spiritual Songs

I will pray with my spirit, but I will also pray with my mind. *I will sing with my spirit,* but I will also *sing with my mind.*

1 Corinthians 14:15

For the first Christians, spiritual songs were free, spontaneous expressions. They arose from their personal, often ecstatic experiences with God. They were performed as solos, with a great deal of improvisation, perhaps on a single syllable of a word such as "alleluia." "Spiritual songs" may be translated literally, "odes on the breath."

The apostle Paul spoke to the church at Corinth about their practice of *praying* and *praising.* His plea was that worship should be a product of the mind and the spirit. *Valid spiritual experiences must always maintain a proper balance between the emotional, spiritual and rational.*

Spiritual songs are the counterpart of today's gospel songs. They are musical expressions of our personal experiences with the Lord, spiritual exhortations to other Christians, or invitations to non-Christians to accept Christ as Savior. The words are subjective or man-centered in character. The music of a gospel song has a more rhythmic emphasis than that of a hymn.

Edmund Simon Lorenz, in his book *Church Music: What a Minister Should Know About It,* defined a gospel song as follows:

A sacred folk song, free in form, emotional in character, devout in attitude, evangelistic in purpose and spirit. These hymns are subjective in the subject matter and develop a single thought, rather than a line of thought. That thought usually finds its supreme expression in the chorus or refrain, which binds the stanzas together in a very close unity just as it does in lyrical poetry, where it is occasionally used.

Sing Spiritual Songs

Gospel music began to flourish in America shortly after the close of the Civil War. It has evolved into a number of popular musical styles. These songs are not meant to be enduring sacred classics, nor are they intended to be the profound teaching hymns of the church. Gospel songs are the "now" expressions of believers, or the "folk music" of the church. These songs give believers an opportunity to express their feelings about God and their religious experiences. A proper balance of gospel songs gives warmth and vitality to the church music ministry.

Therefore, with the apostle Paul we echo, *DON'T NEGLECT THE SINGING OF SPIRITUAL SONGS!*

Write Spiritual Songs

Has God given you a talent for writing words and music? This gift can be used in the church. Original spiritual songs often spark a spiritual renewal among believers. These songs should not be written for profit or to advance a professional reputation, but simply as grateful responses to the indisputable hand of God on the writer's life.

Our hymnals should contain a balance of traditional psalm-classic expressions of praise to the Lord, hymns that teach doctrine, and spiritual songs of Christian experience. It would be good if they also had a section for adding new songs, so that the church hymnal could be a growing collection of new hymns written by members of the congregation. The deep spiritual experiences of believers of the past should be occurring with Christians today, prompting fresh and inspiring musical expressions of the ageless truths of God.

Summary

A New Testament church should always be a singing church, for sacred song is the natural outpouring of joyous Christian hearts. It has often been stated that you can gauge the spiritual atmosphere of a congregation by observing its singing. Nothing is more disheartening to a spirit of public worship than half-hearted, lukewarm singing. The true song of the church, congregational singing, will be an important part of any evangelical church.

Group Discussion

1. What is lost in Christian experience if congregational singing

is excluded? If the music of a church becomes mainly "special music"?

2. Share an experience or reflection from using the church hymnal as part of your personal and family devotions this past week.

3. What suggestions can you offer for the music program of your church to encourage a more significant personal ministry?

4. How would you evaluate the musical balance of styles—psalms, hymns, spiritual songs—used in your church? Give suggestions for improvement.

5. How do you interpret the apostle Paul's instruction to the church of Corinth (1 Corinthians 14:15) regarding praying and singing with the spirit and with understanding?

6. A suggested group project: Prepare a 25-30 minute Sunday evening song service for your church. Develop a theme for this service, but try to have a balance of musical styles involved.

7. A suggested personal project: Try your hand at writing an original spiritual song, such as a short chorus based on some Scripture verse, a spiritual truth, or a recent experience. Share with the group your song and the experience that prompted it.

Reflections

He who knows not the language of praise cannot speak of true happiness. —Unknown

Happiness comes not from having much to live on, but having much to live for. —Unknown

Prayer

Dear God, we thank You for the Bible. Help us to realize more fully the importance of allowing Your Word to have a greater place in our lives. Thank You also for the hymnal and for the men and women through the centuries who have contributed these lofty expressions for our spiritual benefit. We confess that we often sing these great truths with little regard for their meaning. Help us to make a greater use of both the Scriptures and the hymnal in our future church services, as well as in our personal and family devotions. This we pray in Christ's name. AMEN.

6

THE SONG STILLED: THE MIDDLE AGES

We will sing with stringed instruments all the days of our lives in the temple of the Lord.   Isaiah 38:20

Look At History

In addition to first "searching the Scriptures," a second necessary aspect of any serious religious study is surveying history. We learn valuable lessons for the present from the events and experiences of the past.

The next five lessons of *The Endless Song* will be an overview of five periods of time:

The Middle Ages—A.D. 500-1400

   The power and practice of the Medieval Roman Church—the church's song (congregational singing) silenced.

The Renaissance and Protestant Reformation—1400-1600
   The Bible rediscovered and the church's song restored.
The Pietistic and Evangelical Movements—1600-1800
   The church's song revitalized.
The Romantic Period and the American Gospel Hymn—1800-1900
   The era of the gospel song.
The 20th Century—1900 to present
   Contemporary issues and tensions.

For each period we will examine the important people, events, and philosophies that shaped culture and the arts in general, and that influenced the church's music and worship in particular. This brief historical pilgrimage should confirm our conviction that our God is the ruler of the past as well as the Lord of the present and future.

The Medieval Roman Church

Following the decree in 381 that made Christianity the official state religion of Rome, the Christian church experienced phenomenal growth. It was the dominant influence in Western civilization for the next 1000 years. Church buildings known as basilicas, built symbolically in the form of a cross, sprang up throughout Western Europe. Later, larger and more ornate structures, Romanesque and Gothic cathedrals, were built to accommodate expanding congregations.

These buildings were adorned with sculpture and painting. The purpose of these visual arts was not only aesthetic, but also functional—to instruct the masses in the doctrines and dogmas of the church. In the earlier Romanesque churches, the paintings were done in fresh plaster on the walls and ceiling of the church, a form of art known as "fresco." Between 1100-1400, when the great Gothic cathedrals were built, the dominant feature was beautiful stained glass windows. Some of these original windows can still be seen and admired in ancient churches throughout Europe.

The best-known artist of the middle ages was Giotto (c. 1226-1337). His famous work is a monumental fresco of the life of Christ on the walls of the church at Padua, Italy. One of the prominent literary figures of this time was Dante (1265-1321). His epic religious poem, *The Divine Comedy,* gives us a look at life during the middle ages.

In A.D. 787, the Second Council of Nicea issued the following statement about visual arts:

> The substance of religious scenes is not left to the initiative of the artists. It derives from the principles laid down by the Catholic Church and religious tradition. His [the artist's] art belongs to the painter; its organization and arrangement belong to the clergy.

The medieval Roman church became not only the absolute ruler over all spiritual matters, but also dominated the economic, political, social, artistic and cultural life in society as well.

The Church's Liturgy: The Mass

Throughout the early middle ages, religious musical development was limited to a liturgical use in the mass. The church's true song—the singing by lay people—was discontinued. When Latin became the official language of the church's liturgy, and laymen were given almost no part in the service, the worship of the church became "sacerdotal," which means it could only be led by the priesthood. Beginning with the late 2nd century, the Lord's Supper changed from a simple memorial service to an elaborate sacrificial rite known as the eucharist. The liturgy of the mass centered in the eucharist, a commemoration of Christ's sacrifice in which the bread and wine became Christ's body and blood. This doctrine was called transubstantiation, the belief that with the act of consecration by the clergy, the bread and wine were miraculously changed into the actual body and blood of Christ. To receive these elements, then, was to receive Christ.

The Roman Church developed five modes of celebrating the mass, and they were basically unchanged until the Second Vatican Council of 1962. They are:

1. LOW MASS (*missa lecta*). Words spoken quietly by the priest to a silent congregation. Generally celebrated at the small chapels throughout the church.
2. HIGH MASS (*missa cantata*). The primary Sunday or holy day celebration, generally involving a choir.
3. HIGH SOLEMN MASS (*missa solemnis*). For festive occasions. Includes assisting celebrants and generally a choir.
4. PONTIFICAL MASS. A mass in which the pope is personally involved.
5. REQUIEM MASS. A special liturgy for funerals.

For many centuries, the mass inspired many of the choral compositions by master composers of both Catholic and Protestant faiths. Two examples are Bach's "B Minor Mass" and Brahm's "Requiem."

Intoned chants by the clergy, borrowed from the Old Testament, became the foundation of the liturgy of the Mass. Pope Gregory the Great (A.D. 540-604), one of the first church leaders to be seriously concerned about sacred music, did much to improve and organize these chant tunes. His work, "Gregorian Chants," is still the basis of traditional Roman Catholic church music today.

Scholasticism

The philosophy of the later middle ages was known as Scholasticism. This philosophical system sought to harmonize faith and reason on the basis of logic. It organized all human knowledge into seven broad categories, and it systematized the church's means for dispensing grace into seven sacraments. Scholasticism was promoted by the great universities that arose throughout Europe. By the end of the 13th century, some 80 universities had been established. These institutions gradually replaced monasteries in academic importance.

Sacraments

In addition to its liturgy for the mass, the medieval Roman church also developed a system of sacraments. These seven provisions for gaining God's grace are:

1. *Baptism*—the washing away of original sin.
2. *Confirmation*—full admission into the church after instruction.
3. *Penance*—the confession of repeated sins.
4. *Eucharist*—receiving the body of Christ at the mass.
5. *Marriage*—the establishment of a Christian home.
6. *Ordination*—being set apart for the ministry of the church.
7. *Extreme Unction*—a rite to bring God's grace to the dying soul.

Sacred Motets

Beginning in the 9th century, church musicians began adding melodic parts to the chants. The chant or main melody line became known as the *cantus firmus*. This *combining of additional melodic voices to the cantus firmus resulted in polyphonic music, the beginning of harmony.* Polyphony reached its height with the music of Palestrina (1525-1594), an Italian Catholic, and Johann Sebastian Bach (1685-1750), a German Protestant.

This led to a new form of church music: sacred motets. This important form of church music had a Latin text, was unaccompanied, was highly polyphonic in style, and was difficult to sing. Motets still comprise the basis of much church choral music today.

Pipe Organs—The Church's Musical Instrument

The building of magnificent Gothic cathedrals reached its peak during the 13th through the 15th centuries. With their rise came the development of pipe organs and their music. The earliest church organs, dating in the 9th or 10th centuries, were crude instruments. The keys often were three to four inches wide, and were played with the fists. By the 14th century, however, organ music improved greatly, and *organs have since been recognized as the instrument of the church.*

Important Hymnwriters of the Middle Ages

Bernard of Clairvaux (1091-1153). Bernard lived at the height of the Middle Ages, a period of history known as "The Dark Ages." The spiritual and moral darkness of the church had reached a new low. The institution founded by Christ some 1,000 years earlier had become degenerate and corrupt. Many of its prominent leaders lived in flagrant disregard for God's moral laws.

Bernard was born to a noble family in Burgundy, France. His father was a knight and his mother a person of radiant goodness. With his natural charm and talents, Bernard had every opportunity open for a successful secular life. While still in his early twenties, however, Bernard chose the life of a monk at the monastery of Citeaux, France. Within three years his forceful personality, talents, and leadership qualities were recognized, and he was asked to form other branches of this order throughout Europe. During Bernard's lifetime, about 162 similar orders were founded. One of these new monasteries was at Clairvaux, France, where Bernard was made its abbot or head. Here he remained until his death in 1153.

Bernard of Clairvaux represented the best of monastic life. He emphasized personal holiness, simplicity, devotion, prayer, preaching, and ministering to the physical and spiritual needs of mankind. In the 16th century, Martin Luther wrote of Bernard: "He was the best monk that ever lived, whom I admire beyond all the rest put together."

O Sacred Head, Now Wounded

PASSION CHORALE

Attr. to Bernard of Clairvaux, 1091-1153
Trans. by Paul Gerhardt, 1607-1676
Trans. by James W. Alexander, 1804-1859

Hans Leo Hassler, 1564-1612
Har. by Johann Sebastian Bach, 1685-1750

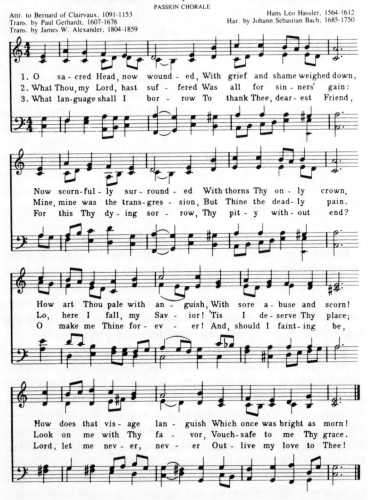

1. O sa-cred Head, now wound-ed, With grief and shame weighed down,
2. What Thou, my Lord, hast suf-fered Was all for sin-ners' gain:
3. What lan-guage shall I bor-row To thank Thee, dear-est Friend,

Now scorn-ful-ly sur-round-ed With thorns Thy on-ly crown,
Mine, mine was the trans-gres-sion, But Thine the dead-ly pain.
For this Thy dy-ing sor-row, Thy pit-y with-out end?

How art Thou pale with an-guish, With sore a-buse and scorn!
Lo, here I fall, my Sav-ior! 'Tis I de-serve Thy place;
O make me Thine for-ev-er! And, should I faint-ing be,

How does that vis-age lan-guish Which once was bright as morn!
Look on me with Thy fa-vor, Vouch-safe to me Thy grace.
Lord, let me nev-er, nev-er Out-live my love to Thee!

Bernard wrote a number of books on such subjects as church government, monasticism, and other church-related topics. He also wrote a number of hymn texts that express a spirit of warmth and devotion to Christ. Many feel that he wrote the 192 line poem, *Dulcis Jesus Memorial* ("Joyful Rhythm on the Name of Jesus").

In the 19th century, Edward Caswell translated portions of this poem into English for a hymn still widely used today, "Jesus, the Very Thought of Thee." This hymn has been translated into more languages than any other hymn except Luther's "A Mighty Fortress Is Our God."

Another important hymn attributed to Bernard is "O Sacred Head, Now Wounded." This text was taken from a lengthy poem, *Rhythmica Oratio*. The poem had seven parts, each addressing various parts of Christ's body—His feet, knees, hands, side, breast, heart, and face—as He suffered on the cross. "O Sacred Head Now Wounded" was adapted from the seventh portion of the poem. It first appeared in English in 1830, after being translated by James W. Alexander, a Presbyterian minister.

Francis of Assisi (1182-1226). "All Creatures of Our God and King" is another inspiring hymn that came from the Middle Ages. This expression of praise, found in nearly every published hymnal today, was originally written in 1225 by one of the most interesting figures in all of church history. Giovanni Bernardone, known to us as Saint Francis of Assisi, was a mystic medieval monk who spent his life as an itinerant evangelist, preaching and helping the poor people of Italy.

Saint Francis was born in Assisi, Italy, in 1182. After an early indulgent life as a soldier, he reformed his ways dramatically at the age of 25. He was determined to serve God by imitating the selfless life of Christ in all that he did. Although his family were people of considerable means, Francis scorned the possession of material goods, denounced his inherited wealth, deprived himself of everything but the most meager necessities, and devoted himself to ministering as Christ's representative. At the age of 28, Francis founded the Franciscan Order of Friars, which developed into a large movement of young men and some women. Francis' preaching consisted of a simple gospel message: "Christ first, Christ last, Christ all and in all." Francis also made much use of singing throughout his ministry; in fact, he often referred to himself as "God's gleeman."

"All Creatures of Our God and King" is taken from one of Saint Francis' writings titled "Canticles of the Sun." Tradition says it was written one hot summer day in 1225, when Francis was blind and terminally ill.

All Creatures of Our God and King

LASST UNS ERFREUEN

Francis of Assisi, 1182-1226
Trans. by William H. Draper, 1855-1933

From *Geistliche Kirchengesäng*, 1623

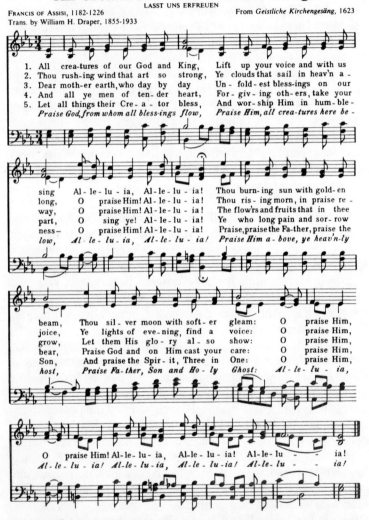

1. All crea-tures of our God and King, Lift up your voice and with us sing   Al - le - lu - ia, Al - le - lu - ia! Thou burn-ing sun with gold-en beam, Thou sil - ver moon with soft - er gleam: O praise Him, O praise Him! Al-le-lu - ia, Al - le - lu - ia! Al-le-lu - - ia!

2. Thou rush-ing wind that art so strong, Ye clouds that sail in heav'n a - long, O praise Him! Al - le - lu - ia! Thou ris - ing morn, in praise re - joice, Ye lights of eve-ning, find a voice: O praise Him,

3. Dear moth-er earth, who day by day Un - fold - est bless-ings on our way, O praise Him! Al - le - lu - ia! The flow'rs and fruits that in thee grow, Let them His glo - ry al - so show: O praise Him,

4. And all ye men of ten - der heart, For - giv - ing oth - ers, take your part, O sing ye! Al - le - lu - ia! Ye who long pain and sor - row bear, Praise God and on Him cast your care: O praise Him,

5. Let all things their Cre - a - tor bless, And wor-ship Him in hum - ble - ness - O praise Him! Al - le - lu - ia! Praise, praise the Fa-ther, praise the Son, And praise the Spir - it, Three in One: O praise Him,

Praise God, from whom all bless-ings flow, Praise Him, all crea-tures here be - low, Al - le - lu - ia, Al - le - lu - ia! Praise Him a - bove, ye heav'n-ly host, Praise Fa-ther, Son and Ho - ly Ghost: Al - le - lu - ia, Al - le - lu - ia! Al - le - lu - ia! Al - le - lu - ia, Al-le - lu-ia! Al-le-lu - - ia!

A familiar verse that has become popular in recent years is this thoughtful prayer, written by St. Francis during his early years:

Lord, make me an instrument of Thy peace. Where there is hatred, let me sow love.
Where there is injury, pardon. Where there is error, truth.
Where there is despair, hope. Where there is sadness, joy.
Where there is darkness, light.

O divine Master, grant that I may not so much seek to be
   consoled, as to console,
To be understood, as to understand. To be loved, as to love.
For it is in giving, that we receive. It is in pardoning, that we
   are pardoned,
It is in dying, that we are born to eternal life.

Important Churchmen of the Middle Ages

Thomas Aquinas (1225-1274). Thomas Aquinas was the most
influential Catholic theologian of the Middle Ages. Many of the
church's doctrines are based on his teachings. They were the result
of his revival and application of Aristotle's writings and principles.
Aquinas taught *that it was the will of man that was corrupted
by the fall, but not his intellect*—promoting the idea *that revelation
and human reason should be treated equally.*

John Wycliffe (1320-1384). John Wycliffe, an Oxford professor,
was one of the first reformers to emphasize the *supreme authority
of the Bible.* He is best remembered for producing an important
English version of the Bible for the common man to read and
understand.

John Hus (1369-1415). John Hus was a professor at the
University of Prague. Strongly influenced by John Wycliffe, he
stressed that *the Bible was man's ultimate authority* in all matters
of faith and practice. Hus was the founder of the Bohemian-
Moravian Church. This group became widely known for their
fervent evangelical spirit, missionary zeal, and congregational
singing. John Hus sang hymns while being burned at the stake
for his beliefs at the Council of Constance, July 6, 1415.

Summary

It is difficult to comprehend that a small, persecuted band of
Christ's followers in the first century would grow to become the
powerful medieval Roman Church, the dominant influence in
Western civilization for more than a millennium.

But this development brought changes in worship, doctrines,
and practices. Most notable was the sacerdotal role of the clergy
at the expense of lay involvement in the worship service. The Bible
became the possession of the clergy alone, who taught that only
they could understand and interpret its meaning. Congregational
singing was stilled. The singing of "psalms, hymns and spiritual
songs" by the people was replaced by the chanting of the clergy,

and later by professional choirs singing sacred motets in Latin. Rather than using music as a vehicle for producing spiritual growth through personal responses from the people, therefore, the church began to promote only artistic music for the enjoyment of society's musical elite.

It should be noted that dramatic changes have occurred in Catholicism following the Second Vatican Council (1962-1965), which released the *Constitution on the Sacred Liturgy.* Today the Scriptures are read repeatedly throughout the Mass liturgy, and laymen are encourged to read the Bible personally. Congregational singing has been given a prominent place in the service, using many of the hymns found in Protestant hymnals. The services now involve lay leaders, and they are conducted in the language of the people. The Vatican Council encouraged worshipers to be "rational, social, and joyful in their services." Many Catholic churches today promote folk music masses as part of their weekly program. After centuries of liturgical staidness, these changes and practices have encouraged a spirit of renewal within the Catholic church. But they have also brought unrest. Older members and traditional ethnic groups are slow to change.

Throughout history, God has always had individuals and groups who accepted His eternal truths and kept singing the endless song. Every generation will have people who are "salt" and "light." This is what Christ promised until His triumphant return to reign as KING OF KINGS, LORD OF LORDS, and THE ETERNAL HEAD OF HIS CHURCH!

Group Discussion

1. What factors do you feel influenced early church leaders to rule against laymen using the Bible and to discourage congregational singing?
2. The underlying meaning of each Catholic Mass is the perpetual commemoration of Christ's atoning sacrifice and the receiving of His saving grace through the consecrated elements. Examine this teaching in the light of Hebrews 6:6; 7:27; 9:11-12; 9:28; 10:11-12; 1 Timothy 2:5.
3. What distinction, if any, do you feel should be made between a church ordinance and a sacrament?
4. In what ways do you feel that lay participation in a worship service demonstrates the important New Testament truth of the priesthood of each believer?

5. In what ways could your church involve the people more in the services?

Reflections

He became what we are in order that we might become as He is. —Athanasius

We are the personification of the things we believe in and for which we would die. —Unknown

When we ask God to do something for us, He generally works to do something in us. —Unknown

Jesus, The Very Thought of Thee

Jesus, the very thought of Thee with sweetness fills my
    breast;
But sweeter far Thy face to see and in Thy presence rest.

No voice can sing, no heart can frame, nor can the
    memory find
A sweeter sound than Thy blest name, O Savior of
    mankind.

O hope of every contrite heart, O joy of all the meek,
To those who fall, how kind Thou art! How good to those
    who seek!

But what to those who find? Ah, this no tongue or pen
    can show;
The love of Jesus, what it is, none but His loved ones
    know.

Jesus, our only joy be Thou as Thou our prize wilt be;
Jesus, be Thou our glory now, and through eternity.
        —Bernard of Clairvaux, 1091-1153
        Translated by Edward Caswall, 1814-1878

Prayer

Dear God, we bless Your name that You are the God of the past as well as our only hope for the future. We are mindful of those believers who preferred death as martyrs rather than acknowledge anyone other than You as Lord. May we with convictions for our beliefs, be a remnant of true believers to keep Your truths alive for this generation. Help us to claim the promise of Scripture that we too can be more than conquerors through Him who loved us. In Christ's name we pray. AMEN.

7

THE SONG RESTORED:
THE PROTESTANT REFORMATION

God is our refuge and strength, a very present help in trouble. Therefore will not we fear...   Psalm 46:1, 2

The Renaissance—Reformation Period

The Reformation occurred simultaneously with the Renaissance, and extended from A.D. 1400 to 1600. The word "renaissance" literally means "rebirth." This was an awakening and flowering of culture, the arts, and learning such as the world had never before experienced. In addition to ushering in vast changes in the fields of art, music, literature, and science, this new spirit also brought far-reaching change in economic, social, political, and religious life.

The philosophy of the Renaissance was a kind of religious humanism—a spirit of individualism, self-confidence, and optimism. Those who had this new spirit believed God gave us this world to enjoy, not that it should be hated to earn future rewards. They also taught that a person should use his intellect and energies to make himself the master of his environment.

Some of the important historical events and influences of the Renaissance period were:

The end of the medieval feudal system and the rise of a middle class; the invention of the printing press in 1454 by Johannes Gütenberg; the development and use of gunpowder; the spirit of exploration for the new world with Columbus, Vasco da Gama, Magellan, and Marco Polo; important advances in science, led by such men as Copernicus (1473-1543) and Galileo (1564-1642); the continued division, weakness, and corruption of the Roman Church; the rise of secular drama to replace the medieval morality plays.

Several of the oustanding artists of the Renaissance were:

Leonardo da Vinci (1452-1519) of Italy; Michelangelo (1475-1564) of Italy; Raphael (1483-1520) of Italy; Titian (1488-1576), Italian/Venetian; Albrecht Durer (1471-1528) of Germany; Jan Van Eyck (1390-1441) of Belgium; El Greco (1541-1614) of Spain.

These artists wanted to use the visual arts to depict beauty for its own sake, not merely as teaching aids for the church. The passion of the Renaissance artist was to develop techniques for achieving perspective and portraying the human body realistically.

The spirit of the Renaissance moved gradually northward from Italy into Germany, France, Switzerland, Holland, and Great Britain. In many of these countries, the concern was not only for a rebirth of culture and the arts, but also the need for a reformed church. *This concern resulted in the 16th century Protestant Reformation Movement.*

Martin Luther (1483-1546). Perhaps the most important day in Protestant history was October 31, 1517. On that date a concerned Augustinian monk, Martin Luther, made his way to the doors of the Cathedral of Wittenberg, Germany, and posted his famous 95 theses (complaints) against the teachings and practices of the medieval Roman Church. In 1520, Pope Leo X issued a Papal Bull condemning the 95 theses, and Luther burned it. The following year Luther was summoned to the Diet of Worms, where he was formally excommunicated from the Catholic church, but he continued to teach, preach, and write. During the years 1521-34, Luther translated the entire Bible into the German language. In 1524, he published the first Protestant hymnal, which contained eight hymns, four of them by Luther. The little book was soon used all over Europe. The exuberant singing of these stately chorale hymns, without accompaniment, became a trademark of the early reformers. Luther's enemies often lamented that the German people were singing themselves into Luther's terrible doctrines, and that his hymns destroyed more souls than all of his writings and sermons.

Basic Tenets of Evangelical Protestantism

The Protestant Reformation movement was built on three main tenets:

1. **The re-establishment of the Scriptures** as sole and ultimate authority for all Christian doctrine and practice. Lay people were encouraged to read and study the Bible for themselves in their own language.

2. **Clarifying the means of salvation.** The reformers taught that persons are made right with God through a personal response of faith to Christ's finished work, *justification by faith alone,* and not through the seven sacraments of the church or by one's good works. They also taught the priesthood of believers: that every believer is a priest before God.

3. **The restoration of congregational singing.** Congregational singing in the liturgy of the mass had been eliminated since the close of the fourth century. Church leaders had decreed that if laymen were not to interpret the Scriptures for themselves, then they also were not to sing the songs of the church. Martin Luther responded forcefully, "Let God speak directly to His people through the Scriptures, and let His people respond with grateful songs of praise." In a real sense, in contrast to the chants of the clergy that formed the musical basis for the Catholic mass, *the praises of the lay people became the musical foundation for Protestant worship.*

In addition, the reformers believed that every Christian, regardless of his vocation, is called to be a personal representative for God. In this view, even the most menial tasks and occupations are sacred trusts. John Calvin often reminded his followers that "working is praying." Before this, the only work that could be considered a sacred calling was a church related vocation.

"A Mighty Fortress Is Our God"

The primary vehicle for popularizing the Reformation was the hymn by Martin Luther referred to earlier, "A Mighty Fortress Is Our God." It is a paraphrase of Luther's favorite psalm, the

46th. The date the hymn was written cannot be determined exactly. Many believe it was written for the Diet of Spires in 1529, when the term "protestant" was first used. The hymn has since been translated and sung in practically every known language around the world.

Although Luther was a theologian, not a musician, he is credited with writing 37 hymns and composing the music for many of them. Luther saw congregational singing as one of the best ways to achieve his spiritual purposes. He stated, "If any would not sing and talk of what Christ has wrought for us, he shows thereby that he does not really believe."

Martin Luther encouraged congregational singing (thus restoring the church's true song), and he followed Roman Catholic tradition by using the choir in the church service. The choir sang the more difficult polyphonic arrangements of the chorale melodies. Luther's musical abilities included a fine tenor voice and a mastery of the flute and the lute.

Luther had a high regard for the ministry of music. He wrote:

Next to the preaching of the Scriptures, I afford music the highest place in the church. I want the Word of God to dwell in the hearts of believers by means of songs.

There is a root-like unity of music and theology. Music is wrapped and locked in theology.

I would allow no man to preach or teach God's people who did not realize the power and use of sacred music.

Other 16th Century Reformers

The revolt against the medieval Roman Church was promoted by a number of individual reformers and groups. Some of them were:

Ulrich Zwingli (1481-1531). Working in Zurich, Switzerland, Zwingli stressed individuality in worship and the absolute authority of the Scriptures. He disagreed with Luther, however, on the meaning and practice of the communion service. Zwingli believed that it represented the congregation's confession of faith in obedience to our Lord's command only, rather than having sacramental significance. Therefore, he felt it should not be a part of every worship service. In his church, Zwingli celebrated communion only four times a year.

Guillaume Farel (1489-1565). A staunch supporter of the sole authority of the Scriptures, he ministered to the French-speaking people in Switzerland.

John Calvin (1509-1564). Calvin reacted more strongly than the other reformers to the teachings and practices of the medieval Roman church. He felt that the others had not gone far enough in their break with the church. When Calvin began his ministry at Geneva, Switzerland, he banned all choral music in the church. He removed the stained glass windows, statues, and icons in the St. Peter's church building. The pulpit and Bible were moved to the forefront of the chancel, symbolizing that the reading and preaching of the Scriptures were the focal points of worship, not the altar.

Calvin published *Institutes of the Christian Religion* in 1536 and revised them in 1559. These writings, with their strong emphasis upon the sovereignty of God, became the basis of reformed theology.

In 1538, John Calvin was exiled to Strasbourg, bordering Germany and France, where he ministered to a congregation of French exiles. Here he became interested in the congregation's singing of the psalms. After writing several psalm versions himself, Calvin commissioned the French court poet, Clement Marot, to set all 150 psalms into meter. This endeavor resulted in the publication in 1562 of the historic *Genevan Psalter.* Few hymnals have influenced Christendom more than this collection.

Calvin held the conviction that "only the Scriptures are worthy to be used in the praise of God." He further instructed his followers to sing the psalms in unison (lest they think about the harmony rather than the words) and without accompaniment. The music editor for the Genevan Psalter was Louis Bourgeois (1510-1561), who adapted tunes from French and German sources, as well as composing some melodies himself. (The tune for the "Doxology" is attributed to him and comes from this *Genevan Psalter.*)

When Calvin returned to Geneva, he used these psalms in worship, singing them in unison but without accompaniment. The Calvinist tradition of psalm-singing was later adopted by the Anglican church and by other Protestant groups, both in England and in America. Some Calvinist groups today still use only the Psalter.

The Anglican Church in England. This church began in 1534 as a result of political rather than doctrinal convictions (the Pope's refusal to sanction King Henry VIII's annulment from Catherine of Aragon). After Henry's death in 1547, Archbishop Cranmer (1489-1556) published in 1549 a reformed English liturgy, *The First Book of Common Prayer.* It taught that worship was to be congregational, not sacerdotal.

John Knox (1505-1572). Strongly Calvinistic in his theology and practice, Knox was the founder of Presbyterianism in England and Scotland.

Other Concerned Groups:

A brief return to Catholicism took place in England during the reign of Queen "Bloody" Mary (1553-1558). During this time, many Protestants either were persecuted or fled to Geneva, where they came under the influence of John Calvin. When they returned to England during the reign of Queen Elizabeth (1558-1603), these leaders promoted the Puritan Movement, which reacted even more strongly to the Catholic church.

This was also the time when the dissenting or non-conformist churches (Presbyterians, Congregationalists, Independents, and Baptists) began to emerge. They sought to reduce worship to its barest simplicity, and to establish a democratic form of church government. Though the Separatist Movement contributed to the cause of Christ, the actions of the more radical factions within this movement will always be a dark blight on church history. Because of the fervent reaction of this group to any semblance of a liturgical church, ancient cathedrals were demolished, stained glass windows broken, artistic ornaments torn down, libraries ransacked, and church organs were destroyed. Martin Luther was strongly opposed to all "anti-liturgy" reaction such as this. He wrote: "Nor am I of the opinion that the gospel should destroy and blight the arts, as some pseudo-religious leaders claim. Rather, I would like to see all of the arts used in the service of Him who gave and made them."

16th Century Catholicism

One of the primary missions of the Catholic church during the early 16th century was the completion of two magnificent structures within the Vatican City, St. Peter's Church and the Sistine Chapel. St. Peter's was begun during the reign of Pope Julius II (1503-1513), whose ambition was to replace the old basilica of St. Peter's with a church so grand that it would "overshadow all of the monuments of ancient imperial Rome." He also wanted to demonstrate to the world once more the greatness of the Catholic church (and to perpetuate his name). The dome for this awe-inspiring building was completed in 1590. The Sistine Chapel, the private chapel of the Pope later called the "exquisite jewel of the Renaissance," was completed in 1481. Michelangelo painted on the ceiling of this lovely structure nine panels representing the chief events in the story of man's redemption, including the popular "The Creation of Man-Adam."

During the latter half of the 16th century, a strong Catholic Counter Reformation took place. This was a serious attempt by some church leaders to purge from the Church the growing influence of the Protestants. Devout leaders such as Ignatius Loyola, founder of the Jesuit Movement, earnestly tried to reform the church from within and to evangelize unchurched areas. However, the Counter Reformation movement eventually led to radical practices such as the Inquisitions.

The best of Catholic church music was produced during this time. The 16th century is often called "The Golden Age of Polyphony" and marks the height of development of the sacred motet. The composer most widely acclaimed for this music was Palestrina.

In 1551, Palestrina came to Rome to become organist and director of the Julian Choir, the performing choir at St. Peter's Church in the Vatican City. The ruling pontiff, Pope Marcellus, died unexpectedly shortly after Palestrina assumed his new position. It is said that Palestrina was so saddened by this event that he desired to compose a perfect musical setting in honor of his beloved pope. This he did, and to this day the "Pope Marcellus Mass" has been considered the standard for all musical settings of the Catholic Mass. Palestrina wrote 100 masses, 200 motets, hymns, offertories, and other liturgical materials. He also provided the music for one of the traditional Easter hymns found in nearly every church hymnal, "The Strife is O'er."

Summary

The Protestant Reformation movement brought vast changes in the worship, doctrines, and practices of the church. The discovery and use of two books, *the Bible and the hymnal,* were major influences in this new church movement.

In addition to the three main bodies of reformers at this time, Lutherans, Calvinists, and Anglicans, other "free" or dissenting groups emerged. These included such non-conformist bodies as

Presbyterians, Congregationalists (Independents), Baptists, and Separatists. The intent of these "free" groups was to move believers away from the liturgical practices and beliefs of "high" churches and to help them become more aware of their personal faith. Sadly, some went to extremes.

The singing of metrical psalms was the dominant form of congregational musical involvement. The transition from psalms to hymns was slow because of strong resistance by traditionalists. The age of the psalter continued until the 18th century, when the writings of Isaac Watts brought a new light to congregational singing. More about that in the next lesson.

Group Discussion

1. Why are the three major emphases that grew out of the Reformation so important?
2. What can we do in this local church to strengthen these Reformation convictions?
3. Discuss the difference between Martin Luther's view of music in the church and that of John Calvin. How is this reflected in the worship services of their followers today?
4. Evangelicals are often criticized for being anti-liturgical and anti-aesthetic. Do you feel that this criticism is justified?
5. What greater role could the arts be given in worship today?
6. What reforms do you feel may be needed in 20th century evangelical Protestantism?
7. If you have ever visited St. Peter's Church, the Sistine Chapel, or one of the other great cathedrals, share your observations.
8. Discuss the meaning and imagery of each verse of "A Mighty Fortress Is Our God." Why do you feel this hymn was such an influence in the 16th century?

Reflections

The Devil, the originator of sorrowful anxieties and restless troubles, flees before the sound of music almost as much as before the Word of God.   —Martin Luther

For the Christian, all of life is sacred—nothing is secular, trivial, or absurd.   —Unknown

The secret of a victorious Christian life is a series of new beginnings.   —Unknown

Faith is learning to live without asking God why. —Unknown

A Mighty Fortress Is Our God

A safe stronghold our God is still, a trusty shield and weapon;
He'll help us clear from all the ill that hath us now o'ertaken.
The ancient prince of hell hath risen with purpose fell;
Strong mail of craft and power he weareth in this hour;
On earth is not his fellow.

With force of arms we nothing can, full soon were we down-
ridden;
But for us fights the proper Man, whom God Himself hath
bidden.
Ask ye who is this same? Christ Jesus is His Name,
The Lord Sabaoth's Son: He, and no other one
Shall conquer in the battle.

And were this world all devils o'er, and watching to devour us,
We lay it not to heart so sore; not they can overpower us.
And let the prince of ill look grim as e'er he will,
He harms us not a whit; for why?—his doom is writ;
A word shall quickly slay him.

God's word, for all their craft and force, one moment will not
linger
But, spite of hell, shall have its course; 'tis written by His finger.
And, though they take our life, goods, honor, children, wife,
Yet is their profit small; these things shall vanish all:
The city of God remaineth.

—Martin Luther, 1483-1546
Translated by Thomas Carlyle, 1795-1881

Prayer

Dear God, Thank You for restoring the song! Thank You for
stalwarts of the past like Martin Luther, John Calvin, and the other
reformers, who kept the truths of the Christian faith alive for us
to know and enjoy today. Like them, help us to be always vigilant
in maintaining the foundations of truth and practice while staying
alert to profitable change. May the authority of Your Word guide
our lives as we seek to communicate the good news of the gospel
to those who desperately need its message. This we pray in our
Savior's name. AMEN.

8

THE SONG REVITALIZED: THE PIETISTIC AND EVANGELICAL MOVEMENTS

Give thanks to the Lord, for He is good; His love endures forever. Let the redeemed of the Lord say this—those He redeemed from the hand of the foe, those He gathered from the lands, from east and west, from north and south.   Psalm 107:1-3

The song of the church, recovered in the Reformation, was given fresh life and new warmth in the years from 1600 - 1900. We will look at these triumphal years of church music in the next two chapters.

The Baroque Period
The years from 1600-1725 are known culturally as the Baroque Period. This was a rich era for the arts, particularly in religious expression. Some historians view this time as the culmination

or fruition of the Protestant Reformation, when society accepted the truth of a transcendent God who had revealed Himself in the Bible.

The arts of this time have three major characteristics. They are: (1) strongly emotional, (2) highly ornamented, and (3) marked by mystical realism. In the visual arts, this period is represented by the Dutch masters Rembrandt (1606-1669), Vermeer (1632-1675), and Van Goyen (1596-1656). A list of other Baroque painters would include these familiar names: Peter Rubens (1577-1640) of Belgium, Nicholas Poussin (1594-1665) of France, and Diego Velazquez (1599-1660) of Spain. René Descartes (1596-1650), the French philosopher, mathematician, and scientist, is referred to as "the father of modern philosophy." The leading literary figures of this time were English writers: John Milton (1608-1674) *Paradise Lost* and Alexander Pope (1688-1744) *The Essay on Man*. In the realm of music, the Baroque period is represented by two giants: George Fredrick Handel (1685-1759) and Johann Sebastian Bach (1685-1750).

Handel, often called "the father of the oratorio" (an oratorio is dramatic music based on a biblical text), began writing the music for his best-known work, *The Messiah,* in 1741. He completed all 53 numbers in just 24 days. *The Messiah* was first performed on April 13, 1742. It is undoubtedly the most highly esteemed and frequently performed oratorio ever written. At the first London performance, when the chorus began the word "Hallelujah," tradition states that King George II was so inspired that he stood to his feet. Audiences still stand today when the first strains of the "Hallelujah" chorus are heard.

Never a deeply religious man, Handel became a different person while composing *The Messiah.* When he had completed the "Hallelujah" chorus, he is said to have responded, "I did think I did see all heaven before me, and the great God Himself." After writing the "Amen" chorus, he told his physician, "I think God has visited me." In all, Handel composed 27 oratorios, including *Israel in Egypt, Belshazzar,* and *Judas Maccabaeus.*

While the German-born Handel became a naturalized English citizen before he was 30 years of age, Johann Sebastian Bach, "God's master musician," never left his native Germany. His entire life was characterized by devotion to God and dedication to the Lutheran church. Bach signed each new composition with the letters "SDG," initials for the Latin phrase, *Soli Deo Gloria,* "For the glory of God alone." Bach's ideal for the church, to integrate music with the spoken word, earned him the title, "the father of church music." To Bach, music and theology were inseparable. He studied the Scriptures seriously throughout his lifetime. His best known works are the *B Minor Mass, Magnificat, St. Matthew Passion, St. John's Passion,* and the *Christmas Oratorio.* He wrote more than 200 cantatas, many of which are still performed today.

The 17th Century Pietistic Movement

Four significant historical events of the 16th and 17th centuries changed the course of church history. *The first* was the Protestant Reformation, dramatized by Martin Luther's posting of the 95 theses at the Cathedral of Wittenberg in 1517.

The second was the influence of the followers of John Hus, the Bohemian martyr burned at the stake in 1415 for his strong evangelical convictions. These zealous believers, known as the Bohemian-Moravian Brethren, lived in present-day Czechoslovakia and Hungary. Many of these Brethren migrated to Germany in search of religious freedom. They were known for their vibrant congregational singing and their missionary concern. They were also noted for the inspiring use of brass instruments in their worship services, a tradition they still follow.

A third important influence on the course of church history was the Thirty Years' War (1618-1648). Germany was the battleground of this drawn-out conflict between warring Catholics and Protestants from various countries throughout Europe. The German nation was reduced to a terrible state of misery. The population dwindled from 16 million to 6 million. Because of the war, however, Protestantism was permanently established throughout northern Europe. Out of this terrible epoch were wrung some of the most noble expressions of praise to God in all hymnody, establishing Germany's reputation as the "home of church music." Heartbreak focused man's attention on God and led to deeper personal religious expression.

The fourth event of these years was the rise within the Lutheran Church of Germany of a movement called *Pietism.* Its leader was a pastor in Frankfort, Philip J. Spener (1635-1705). Using small-cell prayer and Bible study groups, Spener worked to awaken church people who had grown accustomed to the dead orthodoxy that had already overtaken the state Lutheran church. He called for a "religion of the heart"—a personal faith in Christ and an awareness of the demands that faith makes on the believer for holy Christian living. A stirring praise hymn, "Sing Praise to God Who Reigns Above," is a product of this movement.

These above four important influences produced a great wealth of excellent German hymns. These hymns were more subjective and passionate than the earlier Lutheran chorale hymns.

Now Thank We All Our God
NUN DANKET

MARTIN RINKART, 1586-1649
Trans. by Catherine Winkworth, 1827-1878

JOHANN CRÜGER, 1598-1662

1. Now thank we all our God With hearts and hands and voic - es,
2. O may this boun-teous God Thru all our life be near us,
3. All praise and thanks to God The Fa - ther now be giv - en,

Who won-drous things hath done, In whom His world re - joic - es;
With ev - er joy - ful hearts And bless - ed peace to cheer us;
The Son and Him who reigns With Them in high-est heav - en—

Who from our moth-ers' arms Hath blessed us on our way
And keep us in His grace, And guide us when per - plexed,
The one e - ter - nal God Whom earth and heav'n a - dore—

With count - less gifts of love, And still is ours to - day.
And free us from all ills In this world and the next.
For thus it was, is now, And shall be ev - er - more.

"Now Thank We All Our God"

This familiar thanksgiving hymn, a direct result of the Thirty Years' War, was written shortly before its close. With the exception of Martin Luther's "A Mighty Fortress Is Our God," no hymn has been used more widely in German churches than "Now Thank We All Our God."

The hymn's author, Martin Rinkart (1586-1649), was a Lutheran pastor in the village of Eilenberg. He arrived there at the age of 31, just as the war was starting. Rinkart spent the remaining 32 years of his life ministering to these suffering people. Because Eilenberg was a walled city, it became an overcrowded refuge for political and military fugitives. Throughout the war, several waves of deadly disease and famine swept the city. Armies marched through the town, leaving death and destruction behind. The Rinkart home served as a refuge for victims, even though Rinkart often had difficulty providing for his own family.

The plague of 1637 was particularly severe. At its height, Rinkart was the only minister who stayed behind to care for the sick and dying. He conducted as many as 50 funeral services per day, even helping to dig the graves. Most of the members of his immediate family died during this time. Yet, amazingly enough, with all of his responsibilities and problems, Rinkart was a prolific writer and a musician. He wrote seven dramatic productions about the events of the Reformation and a total of 66 hymns.

17th Century Developments in England

Following the publication of the *Genevan Psalter,* nearly 100 psalters were published in the next century. This period is called "the age of the psalter." In Great Britain, one of the most notable was *The Whole Book of Psalms, Collected into Englysh Metre,* by T. Sternhold, Hopkins and others, 1562. This psalter and the *Book of Common Prayer,* containing the ritual of the Anglican Church, formed the basis of public worship. Other important psalters included *The Scottish Psalter* in 1564, under the leadership of John Knox; the *Thomas Este's Psalter* in 1592, a significant publication because it first used specific names for tunes; and the *Thomas Ravenscroft Psalter* in 1621, important because it attempted to collect all existing psalm tunes into one volume.

In addition to the congregational singing of these metrical versions of the psalms, the 17th century gave rise to the English anthem for church choirs. *The Prayer Book* of 1662 states that "anthems are to be considered a regular part of worship in churches which boasted a choir." English anthems are a counterpart to the Latin sacred motets used in Catholic churches. Anthems are still used in many Protestant churches today. The leading composer of English anthems during the 17th century was Henry Purcell (1658-1695).

The United States

In America, the early settlers used the same psalters they had used in England. They clung to the idea that God would be insulted if men offered praise to Him with any words other than those He had dictated in the Scriptures. The Puritans of Salem used the *Sternhold and Hopkins Psalter,* while the Pilgrims at Plymouth brought the *Ainsworth Psalter.* Within a few years after their arrival, however, the Puritans published their own psalter, *The Book of Psalms Faithfully Translated Into English Meter,* 1640. This book, commonly known as the *Bay Psalm Book,* was the first book published in the American colonies. This psalter enjoyed widespread popularity and appeared in 27 editions. The ninth edition in 1698 was the first to include music with the words. It consisted of 13 melodies that fit the meter of all 150 Psalms.

An interesting technique used by the congregations of this time was the practice of "lining out" the psalm to be sung. Due to the lack of music, each church appointed a deacon to "line out" the psalm. He would read and sing the words of a line of music; then the congregation would imitate the line. Sometimes it would take as long as 30 minutes to complete the singing of one psalm. It was also the deacon's responsibility to give the proper pitch and to keep the congregation on the right tune. Any type of lively music was thought by the Puritans to be of the devil. This tedious, uninspired style of congregational singing eventually led to the decline of psalm-singing in America. It paved the way in the 18th and 19th centuries for the gradual acceptance of the "human composure" hymns of Watts, Wesley, and other English hymnwriters. The transition from unaccompanied congregational singing to the use of "mechanical music" such as pump organs also met resistance in this country. Some worshipers viewed the organ as "the devil's box of whistles."

Isaac Watts

Isaac Watts (1674-1748) brought a new epoch of congregational singing to England that eventually spread to the United States. At an early age, Watts became concerned with the dismal state of congregational singing. So he wrote new metrical versions of the psalms, with a concern for "christianizing them with the New Testament message and style." In 1719, he published *The Psalms of David Imitated in the Language of the New Testament and Applied to the Christian State and Worship.* Some of Watts' paraphrases based on psalm settings are still used today: "Jesus Shall Reign," Psalm 72; "O God, Our Help in Ages Past," Psalm 90; "Joy to the World," Psalm 98.

Isaac Watts, a Congregationalist, was fervently Calvinistic in doctrine. He not only united Hebrew and Christian ideals with his new metrical psalmody, but he also believed that writers should be free to express praise and devotion to God in their own words. These texts became known as "hymns of human composure." Among Watts' 600 hymns are "When I Survey the Wondrous Cross," "I Sing the Mighty Power of God," and "Am I a Soldier of the Cross?" He became known as "the father of English hymnody."

The Classical Period

The following years in the history of culture (1725-1800) are called the Classical Period. In philosophy, this span is known as the *"Enlightenment," the Age of Reason,"* and *"Rationalism."* Philosophers and writers such as Voltaire (1694-1778) and Rousseau (1712-1778) promoted statements like these: "There is nothing in the world but what the senses can perceive and reason apprehend—nothing but scientific fact." "Man no longer has a need for God."

This renewed humanistic emphasis was marked by a spirit of revolution. It contributed to the English "bloodless revolution" of 1688, the American Revolution of 1776-1783, and the French Revolution in 1789-1799. Uprisings also occurred in Ireland, the Low Countries, Hungary, Poland, and parts of Switzerland.

Important artists of the 18th century were Antoine Watteau (1684-1721) of France; Jacques Louis David (1748-1825) of France; William Hogarth (1697-1764) of England; Thomas Gainsborough (1727-1788) of England; and Francisco Goya (1746-1828) of Spain.

Musically, the Classical Period is best represented by three noted composers: Franz Joseph Haydn (1732-1809); Wolfgang Amadeus Mozart (1756-1791); and Ludwig Van Beethoven (1770-1827).

This was the period of new musical forms—symphonies, string quartets, and operas. The ideal of the Classical Period composers was to achieve a perfection of form and structure in their compositions. Though Haydn, Mozart, and Beethoven wrote primarily secular music, they contributed important sacred works as well. The most familiar are Haydn's oratorio, *The Creation;* Mozart's *Requiem:* and Beethoven's oratorio, *The Mount of Olives.* Some hymn texts were adapted to their music: "Glorious Things of Thee Are Spoken" by Haydn; "Jesus, I My Cross Have Taken" by Mozart; and "Joyful, Joyful We Adore Thee" by Beethoven.

The 18th Century Evangelical Awakening

The 18th century was a period of moral degeneration. The lifestyle of the European aristocracy and nobility was represented by the artistic term "rococo," a culture expressed in lighthearted frivolity, superficiality, ultra-refinement, and sensuousness. The characteristic motif of Rococo art was the delicate scroll of the seashell. Society's lower classes, however, lived in poverty, cruelty, ignorance, and vulgarity. State churches had become more and more corrupt and had little concern for individual welfare. Even the dissenting or non-conformist free churches had become cold, institutionalized, and non-evangelistic.

The evangelical awakening took place in this setting. Individual leaders were motivated by a zealous desire to confront the unreached masses outside of the church with the need for a personal relationship with Christ. The following influences aided the movement:

1. *The beginning of the Sunday School.* In Gloucester, England, Robert Raikes (1736-1811) began taking off the streets children who were being exploited with such abuses as child labor. Raikes taught them to read and to understand the message of the Bible. Following the close of the American Revolutionary War in 1783, the Methodists promoted the cause of religious education with children, and in 1824 the American Sunday School Union was organized.

2. *The beginning of the foreign missionary movement.* William Carey (1761-1834), England, was the pioneer in foreign missions. Carey established the Baptist Missionary Society in 1792, and the following year he left for India. Numerous missionary organizations were founded in the next few years, including the famous London Missionary Society in 1795.

3. *The Revival movement in England and the United States*. The most important revivalists were: John Wesley (1703-1791), Charles Wesley (1708-1788), George Whitefield (1714-1770), Jonathan Edwards (1703-1758).

Charles Wesley

The Wesleyan Movement was the spark that set off the great revivals. The hearty singing introduced by the Wesleys helped them reach the unchurched with the gospel. Together, John (the preacher) and Charles (the musician) wrote and translated approximately 6,500 hymn texts. Their theology was Arminian (an emphasis upon man's free will), contradicting the Calvinistic "election" emphasis of the Isaac Watts' hymns. The Wesleys wrote with warmth and conviction on nearly every phase of Christian experience. Some of Charles Wesley's hymns we sing today are: "O For a Thousand Tongues to Sing," "And Can It Be?" "Soldiers of Christ Arise," "A Charge to Keep I Have," "Depth of Mercy," "Hark! The Herald Angels Sing," "Christ the Lord Is Risen Today," and "Jesus, Lover of My Soul."

Other 18th Century Hymnwriters

In addition to Watts and Wesley, the 18th century produced these English hymn writers: Joseph Addison (1672-1719), "When All Thy Mercies, O, My God"; Philip Doddridge (1702-1751), "O Happy Day That Fixed My Choice"; William Williams (1717-1781), "Guide Me, O Thou Great Jehovah"; Thomas Olivers (1725-1799), "The God of Abraham Praise"; Augustus Toplady (1740-1778), "Rock of Ages, Cleft for Me"; Edward Perronet (1721-1792), "All Hail the Power of Jesus' Name"; John Newton (1725-1807), "Amazing Grace"; William Cowper (1731-1800), "God Moves in a Mysterious Way"; John Fawcett (1739-1817), "Blest Be the Tie That Binds"; George Heath (1745-1822), "My Soul, Be On Thy Guard." Hymn texts of this era whose authors are unknown are: "Come, Thou Almighty King," "How Firm a Foundation," and "Praise the Lord! Ye Heavens Adore Him."

The hymnwriters of the 18th century were primarily concerned with using the words of their hymns to promote a particular doctrine. These authors were usually ministers who prepared their hymn texts to conclude or reinforce a sermon. For this reason, *18th century hymns are often called the "doctrinal hymns of the church."*

"Rock of Ages"

This 18th century hymn was born in a spirit of passionate theological controversy. It was written by Augustus Toplady just two years before his early death in 1778. After his conversion to Christ at the age of 16, young Toplady was attracted to the ministry of John and Charles Wesley. As time went on, however, he became an avid proponent of the "election" doctrines of John Calvin. With public debates, pamphlets, and sermons, Toplady and John Wesley carried on theological warfare.

Following are several of their recorded statements:

Toplady—I believe him [John Wesley] to be the most rancorous hater of the gospel system that appeared in this Island. . .Wesley is guilty of Satanic shamelessness. . .of uniting the sophistry of a Jesuit with the authority of a pope.

Wesley—I dare not speak of the deep things of God in the spirit of a prize fighter or a stage player, and I do not fight with chimney sweeps.

The text of "Rock of Ages" contains obvious satirical swipes at the Wesleys' emphasis on the need for contrite repentance. Note Toplady's rebuttal in the second stanza:

Could my tears forever flow, could my zeal no languor know,
These for sin could not atone—Thou must save, and Thou alone.

Despite the belligerent intent behind this text, God in His providence has chosen to preserve the hymn for the past 200 years so that both Calvinistic and Arminian congregations can sing it with spiritual profit and blessing.

Instructions For Singing

With the increased involvement of the people in singing hymns, church leaders were concerned about congregational participation. John Wesley gave these instructions for church members:

SING ALL. See that you join with the congregation as frequently as you can.
SING LUSTILY, and with good courage. Beware of singing as if you were half-dead or half-asleep, but lift up your voice with strength.
SING MODESTLY. Do not bawl, so as to be heard above or distinct from the rest of the congregation—that you may not

destroy the harmony—but strive to unite your voices together so as to make one clear melodious sound.

Above all, *SING SPIRITUALLY.* Have an eye to God in every word you sing. Aim at pleasing Him more than yourself, or any other creature.

Jonathan Edwards wrote these strong words about singing:

As it is the command of God that all should sing, so all should make conscience of learning to sing, as it is a thing which cannot be decently performed without learning; those, therefore, who neglect to learn to sing live in sin as they neglect what is necessary in order to their attending to one of the ordinances of God's worship.

Summary

The 17th and 18th centuries were marked by two important spiritual movements, pietism and evangelicalism. The Pietistic Movement took place within the church and sought to revive believers through personal Bible study, prayer, and personal growth. The Evangelical Awakening was an effort to reach individuals outside of the church with the gospel. With both of these movements, as with the Protestant Reformation, the singing of the people was important.

Group Discussion

1. Do you feel there is a relationship between the culture—art, literature, drama, and music—of any historical period and the general moral and spiritual climate of that period? Relate to the 17th and 18th centuries.

2. What is your personal response to the word "pietism" or the concept of a "pious" individual? Can you redefine this term into a more relevant 20th century concept?

3. What does the word "evangelical" mean to you? What do you feel are the essential beliefs and practices necessary for any individual or church to identify itself as "evangelical"?

4. Why do you feel the 18th century Evangelical Awakening began during times of moral and spiritual degeneracy? Why does the church so often minister most effectively during periods of adversity and persecution?

5. One of the important characteristics of the evangelical movement is its emphasis upon the Sunday School. Discuss and evaluate this particular ministry in your church.

6. Analyze the words of an 18th century hymn such as "Rock of Ages" and discuss its doctrine.

7. Discuss the instructions and advice given by John Wesley and Jonathan Edwards for improving congregational singing. Do you feel that this still applies today?

Reflections

The Christian life that is joyless is a discredit to God and a disgrace to itself.   —Maltbie D. Babcock

The aim and final reason for all music should be nothing else but the glory of God and the refreshment of the spirit.—J. S. Bach

How Firm a Foundation

How firm a foundation, ye saints of the Lord, is laid for your faith in His excellent Word!

What more can He say than to you He hath said, to you, who for refuge to Jesus have fled.

"Fear not, I am with thee, O be not dismayed; for I am thy God, I will still give thee aid;

I'll strengthen thee, help thee, and cause thee to stand, upheld by my gracious omnipotent hand.

"When through fiery trials thy pathway shall lie, My grace, all sufficient, shall be thy supply.

The flame shall not hurt thee; I only design thy dross to consume and thy gold to refine.

"The soul that on Jesus hath leaned for repose, I will not, I will not desert to his foes;

That soul, though all hell should endeavor to shake, I'll never, no never, no never forsake!"

—From John Rippon's *Selection of Hymns, 1787*

Prayer

Dear God, we give thanks for Your leading through history. We see Your hand of guidance as we reflect on the past. We are grateful for those leaders who kept alive the truth that man's standing with You must be based on a personal relationship. May the integrity of the gospel message never become distorted and misunderstood by unbelievers today because of our disobedient or shallow living. Help us to know ourselves as You know us. In the name of our victorious Savior, we pray. AMEN.

9
THE NEW SONG:
AMERICAN GOSPEL HYMNS

Sing joyfully to the Lord, you righteous; it is fitting for the upright to praise Him. Praise the Lord with the harp; make music to Him on the ten-stringed lyre. Sing to Him a new song; play skillfully, and shout for joy. For the word of the Lord is right and true; He is faithful in all He does.   Psalm 33:1-4

Romanticism

The 19th century is known as the "Age of Romanticism." This period emphasized emotional freedom in the arts. It was a revolt against the disciplines and restraints of 18th century classicism. The Romantic artists wanted to express themselves as they pleased. This "cult of feeling" allowed anything capable of arousing an intense emotional response. Therefore, liberty, power, love, the exotic, and the bizarre soon became the subject matter of artistic expressions in literature, drama, art, and music.

Here are some of the important events and influences during this time:

Power looms for cotton gins, 1785; Monroe Doctrine, 1823; American Civil War, 1861-1865; the long reign of Queen Victoria in England, 1837-1901; the rule of Napoleon I (1769-1821) and his nephew, Napoleon III (1808-1873); the unification of Italy in 1870 and Germany in 1871; internal combustion engines, 1876; development of steel, 1880; telephone, 1876; telegraph, 1889; diesel engines, 1893; Model T Ford cars, 1900; first powered plane flight, 1903.

The 19th century also witnessed the rise of communism. Karl Marx (1818-1883) published the "Communist Manifesto" in 1848, and his theory was developed by Lenin (1870-1924). This century also gave rise to Sigmund Freud (1856-1939), the Austrian psychologist. He taught that man's behavior is the result of his subconscious mind, and that all behavior is directly motivated by three basic drives: power, self-preservation, and sex. John Dewey (1859-1952), American philosopher and educator, was a pragmatist. He taught that anything that produces results is truth. The 19th century was the heyday of science. Charles Darwin (1809-1882) promoted the theories of natural evolution. His *Origin of the Species* was published in 1862.

In the United States, the period after the Civil War (1861-1865) was filled with social upheaval and change. The issues resulting from the Union victory, the impact of the industrial revolution, and the influx of a flood of immigrants were being worked out.

The important painters of this era were:

France: Theodore Gericault, 1791-1824. One of the first to paint highly emotional themes. Eugene Delacroix, 1798-1863. A strong leader of the revolutionary spirit. Paul Gauguin, 1848-1903. Spent most of his later years seeking reality in the primitive South Sea island of Tahiti.

Spain: Francisco Goya, 1746-1828. Depicted the moral conditions of his country and of the Catholic church.

England: William Blake, 1757-1828. A writer as well as a painter; he tried to render visible the mysteries of the supernatural world.

United States: Winslow Homer, 1836-1910. One of the first American artists to receive international recognition.

Leading 19th century composers were:

Germany: Ludwig Van Beethoven, 1770-1827. Considered a "transition" between the Classical and Romantic styles. Robert Schumann, 1810-1856. Wrote exclusively for the piano. Felix Mendelssohn, 1809-1847. Composer of two important oratorios,

Elijah and *St. Paul*. Johannes Brahms, 1833-1897. Composed
the famous *Requiem*. Richard Wagner, 1813-1883. Composed
operas.
Austria: Franz Schubert, 1797-1828. Composed German art songs.
Poland: Frederick Chopin, 1810-1849. Composed piano music.
Italy: Giuseppe Verdi, 1813-1901. Composed operas.

Romanticism reached its zenith from 1870-1890 with a style of
painting and music called *Impressionism*. This rather vague,
abstract expression was best represented in the works of two
French painters: Claude Monet (1840-1926) and Auguste Renoir
(1841-1919). Parallel expressions in music were the compositions
of Claude Debussy (1862-1918), also from France. Debussy tried
to reflect in music the ethereal qualities of the Impressionist
painters. Impressionism was important, not only as the culmination
of the Romantic Movement, but also because it served as a
transition into the art and music of the 20th century.

Hymn Developments in England
We noted earlier that many of the hymnwriters of the late 17th
and 18th centuries used the words of their compositions to promote
their doctrinal convictions. Often their poetry was rather crude.
By contrast, 19th century hymnists, influenced by the spirit of
the Romantic Age, raised the literary quality of their hymns.
The leading hymnwriters of England during this period were:
Reginald Heber (1783-1826). "Holy, Holy, Holy"
Henry Francis Lyte (1793-1847). "Abide With Me"
Sir John Bowring (1792-1872). "In The Cross of Christ I Glory"
Sir Robert Grant (1779-1838). "O Worship the King"
Charlotte Elliott (1789-1871). "Just As I Am"
Frances Ridley Havergal (1836-1878). "Take My Life and Let
It Be"

The Oxford Movement began in England in 1833. It was an
attempt to make the Anglican Church even more liturgical, even
more "high church." It was a reaction to the "looseness" within
the church caused by the evangelical influence, with its emphasis
upon the individual and the need for personal conversion. During
this time a number of prominent Anglican leaders left the state
church to become leaders within Catholicism. In 1861, the Oxford
Movement produced one of the most important hymnbooks ever
published, *Hymns Ancient and Modern*. One of its purposes was

to rediscover hymns of Greek and Latin origin dating before the Reformation and to translate them into English. Important hymnwriters of the Oxford Movement were:

John Henry Newman (1801-1890), Catholic. "Lead, Kindly Light"
Frederick Faber (1814-1863), Catholic. "Faith of Our Fathers"
Edward Caswall (1814-1878), Catholic. "May Jesus Christ Be
    Praised"
John Mason Neale (1818-1866). "O Come, O Come Emmanuel"

(Neale remained in the Anglican Church to become the leading translator of pre-Reformation Greek and Latin hymns).

Developments In America

Following the "Great Awakening," spearheaded by Jonathan Edwards and aided by English evangelist, George Whitefield, America experienced another significant revival in the early 19th century. It began under the leadership of James McGready, a Presbyterian preacher in Logan County, Kentucky. This revival, stirring the entire South, centered in large outdoor services known as "camp meetings." Thousands of people would make a 3 to 4 day journey by wagon, or as much as a week's journey by foot, to attend. The worshipers brought tents, bedding, and food to last for several days. The services were held in the open air. The people lived in their wagons or in temporary "brush arbor" camps.

An important aspect of these meetings was the singing. They used unique songs that became known as "camp meeting hymns." These songs expressed simple truths about personal salvation and the prospect of heaven. The tunes, often borrowed from popular secular tunes of the day, were easily learned and sung from memory. They generally had a "catchy" refrain that could generate mass enthusiasm, resulting in foot tapping, body swaying, and hand clapping. The leader of the singing was "the preacher with the loudest voice."

From these revival meetings came a large repertory of folk hymns and spiritual songs. Itinerant singing teachers, enterprising ministers, and publishers compiled and commercialized these songs into such well-known hymnals as *The Kentucky Harmony, The Southern Harmony,* and *The Sacred Harp.* An important feature of these books was the use of shaped notes to aid in sightreading. The following shaped notes were used:

△	▽	◇	▷	○	□	♡	△
do	re	mi	fa	so	la	ti	do

About the same time came other folk songs, the Negro spirituals. Their words were plaintive expressions of the soul. An example is "Nobody Knows the Trouble I've Seen." The spirituals were an outgrowth of an active evangelical ministry among the blacks at the close of the 18th and in the early years of the 19th century.

Another important revival movement occurred in the early and mid-19th century in the established churches along the Eastern seaboard. It was led by Charles Grandison Finney (1792-1875), a trained lawyer and an ordained Presbyterian minister. Perhaps the greatest of American revivalists, Finney was known for his ability to "encourage the saints and scare the sinners" with prolonged and persuasive invitations. His emphasis on an instantaneous conversion experience was a marked contrast to the more Calvinistic evangelists, who gave greater stress to a process of conversion. Finney spent his later years as a professor of theology and also as President of Oberlin College.

Finney's music associate for many of these crusades was Thomas Hastings (1779-1852), who wrote the music for such favorite hymns as "Rock of Ages," "From Every Stormy Wind That Blows," and "Majestic Sweetness Sits Enthroned." Though his formal musical training was meager, and as an albino he was afflicted with eye problems throughout his life, Hastings composed approximately 1,000 hymn tunes and authored more than 600 hymn texts. The Finney-Hastings meetings marked the first use of song books published specifically for revivals. Along with Lowell Mason, Thomas Hastings is generally credited with being the person most influential in shaping the development of church music in the United States during the 19th century.

Other Important Influences

In addition to these 18th and 19th century revival movements, other important influences contributed to the development of American gospel hymnody. These include: the efforts of Lowell Mason, the ministry of the Sunday School, the work of the YMCA, a concern for foreign missions, and the mass evangelistic crusades of D. L. Moody.

Lowell Mason. The work of Lowell Mason (1792-1872) was especially important in the early development of American music. He expanded the singing schools established by 18th century itinerant musicians into full-fledged Normal Schools that trained teachers for public school music. It was Mason, more than anyone else, who persuaded school authorities that the moral power of music is essential to the well-being of children. Music education was first introduced into the public school curriculum in 1838. Mason also profoundly influenced sacred music, and he is often called "the father of American church music." He did much to train and organize church choirs, and he encouraged congregational singing with the writing of approximately 700 hymn tunes. He composed the music for these hymns: "Nearer My God to Thee," "When I Survey the Wondrous Cross," "Joy to the World," and "My Faith Looks Up to Thee."

Sunday School Movement. A second important influence in the development of 19th century American church music was the growing effort to evangelize children through the Sunday School movement. Hundreds of religious songs were written that would be enjoyable to children and at the same time would teach them spiritual truths. During this period many Sunday School hymnals were published. These songs became favorites with adults as well as children. William B. Bradbury (1816-1868) was a pioneer in music for children, both for the church and in the public schools of New York. In addition to composing the music for the all-time favorite hymn of children everywhere, "Jesus Loves Me," Bradbury also contributed the music for "The Solid Rock," "Sweet Hour of Prayer," "He Leadeth Me," and "Just As I Am."

YMCA (Young Men's Christian Association) A third influence on the American gospel hymn movement was the founding of the YMCA, first in England in 1844 and later in the United States in 1851. In its early days, this organization sponsored large religious conventions. Its daily interdenominational noon-day prayer meetings were also popular. These services were marked by enthusiastic group singing of newer spiritual songs.

Foreign Missions. A fourth influence in the development of American gospel hymnody was the rise of foreign missions. New missionary societies were being formed, such as the Baptist Missionary Society, by William Carey in 1792. Hymnwriters were quick to respond by writing hymns to challenge Christian young people with foreign missionary service.

Mass Evangelism. The climax of the gospel song development occurred during the last quarter of the 19th century. It centered in the ministries of men like Dwight L. Moody (1837-1899), who conducted mass evangelistic crusades in the United States and

Great Britain. Revival fires were also stirring in Scandinavia and parts of Europe. During the Swedish revival, for example, Lina Sandell (1832-1903), often called "the Fanny Crosby of Sweden," wrote many gospel favorites.

Two of her hymns are "Day by Day" and "More Secure Is No One Ever."

Two Americans besides Moody deserve recognition: Ira D. Sankey (1840-1908) and Fanny J. Crosby (1820-1915). This trio— Moody, the evangelist; Sankey, the musician and publisher; Fanny Crosby, the prolific songwriter—did much to promote the spread of the American gospel song.

The Gospel Song

In America emerged a new type of sacred music known as the "gospel song." The singing of psalms, hymns, and spiritual songs had been an important part of public worship since the Protestant Reformation. Ira Sankey, in his evangelistic campaigns with Mr. Moody, introduced a new style of sacred songs that were *"calculated to awaken the careless, to melt the hardened, and to guide inquiring souls to Jesus Christ."*

Many authors have attempted to define the gospel song and to distinguish it from more liturgical hymns. Look at these contrasting elements:

Liturgical Traditional Hymns	*Gospel Song Hymns*
1. Primary purpose is to glorify one or all of the persons of the Godhead. Generally more objective and vertical in character.	1. Primary purpose is to give a testimony, an exhortation, a warning, or an invitation. Generally subjective and horizontal in character.
2. Used primarily for Christians in a worship service.	2. Used primarily in evangelistic, revival, and fellowship services.
3. Music is stately, dignified and devotional in character. Harmonically, the songs are characterized by frequent chord changes.	3. Music is usually rhythmically fast or lilting, generating a pervasive enthusiasm. Harmonically, the songs are characterized by few chord changes.

4. Notes of even time value. Comparatively few eighth or sixteenth notes.

4. Notes of varied time value, with dotted notes ♪.♪ - ♩♪ predominant. The use of lilting 6/8 rhythm is common.

5. Progresses in thought from one stanza to the next without the use of a refrain or chorus.

5. The thought of each stanza finds its supreme expression in the refrain or chorus.

Three Gospel Song Favorites

Many gospel songs were written in the heat of some sudden inspiration or as a result of a dramatic human experience. Here are the stories of three of the more well-known:

"The Ninety and Nine"
Words by Elizabeth C. Clephane (1830-1869)
Music by Ira D. Sankey (1840-1908)

Ira D. Sankey gave this account of the birth of his song:

Mr. Moody and I were riding in a train one morning from Glasgow to Edinburgh, Scotland, to conduct a service in the Free Assembly Hall of Edinburgh. I stopped to purchase a newspaper in the train depot, hoping to get some news from America. While reading the paper during the ride, I discovered a most interesting poem written for children by a Scottish woman named Elizabeth Clephane. I tried to show the poem to Mr. Moody, but he was too busy preparing his sermon. Finally, I simply cut out the poem and placed it in my vest pocket.

At the meeting that afternoon in Edinburgh, the subject of Moody's message was "The Good Shepherd," based on the account in Luke 15. Finishing his sermon, Mr. Moody suddenly announced, "Mr. Sankey will now sing an appropriate closing number."

Startled, I could recall nothing that seemed appropriate. Then I remembered the little poem that I had put in my vest pocket. I placed the newspaper clipping on the folding organ before me, breathed a prayer for divine help, struck the chord of A flat, and began to sing the words. Note by note the tune was given, and that same tune with those words has remained unchanged to the present time.

As I neared the end of the song, Mr. Moody was in tears and so was I. When he arose to give the invitation for salvation, many lost sheep responded to the call of Christ. It was one of the most intense and inspiring moments of my entire life.

It Is Well With My Soul

HORATIO G. SPAFFORD, 1828-1888   PHILIP P. BLISS, 1838-1876

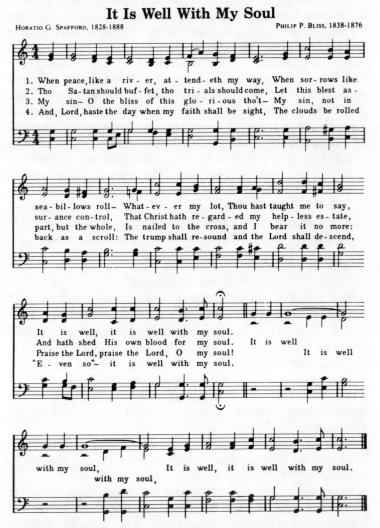

1. When peace, like a riv - er, at - tend - eth my way, When sor - rows like
2. Tho Sa - tan should buf - fet, tho tri - als should come, Let this blest as -
3. My sin— O the bliss of this glo - ri - ous tho't— My sin, not in
4. And, Lord, haste the day when my faith shall be sight, The clouds be rolled

sea - bil - lows roll— What - ev - er my lot, Thou hast taught me to say,
sur - ance con - trol, That Christ hath re - gard - ed my help - less es - tate,
part, but the whole, Is nailed to the cross, and I bear it no more:
back as a scroll: The trump shall re - sound and the Lord shall de - scend,

It is well, it is well with my soul. It is well
And hath shed His own blood for my soul. It is well
Praise the Lord, praise the Lord, O my soul! It is well
"E - ven so"— it is well with my soul.

with my soul, It is well, it is well with my soul.
with my soul,

As a young man, Horatio Spafford had established a successful legal practice in Chicago. Despite his financial success, Spafford always maintained a keen interest in Christian activities. He enjoyed a close and active relationship with D. L. Moody and the other evangelical leaders of that era.

Some months before the Chicago fire of 1871, Spafford had invested heavily in real estate on the shore of Lake Michigan. His holdings were wiped out by the fire. Shortly before this, he had experienced the death of his only son. Desiring a rest for his wife and four daughters, as well as wishing to assist Moody and Sankey in one of their campaigns in Great Britain, Spafford planned a European trip for his family in 1873. In November of that year, because of unexpected last-minute business developments, he had to remain in Chicago. He sent his wife and four daughters ahead as scheduled on the *S.S. Ville du Harve.* He expected to follow in a few days. On November 22 the ship was struck by the *Lochearn,* an English vessel, and sank in 12 minutes. Several days later the survivors were finally landed at Cardiff, Wales. Mrs. Spafford cabled her husband, "Saved alone." Shortly afterward he left by ship to join his bereaved wife. It is speculated that on the sea near the area where it was thought that his four daughters died, Spafford penned the words that described his personal grief: "When sorrows like sea billows roll...".

"Blessed Assurance"
Mrs. Joseph Knapp, an amateur musician and close friend of Fanny Crosby, had just entered Fanny Crosby's home in New York.

"Oh, Fanny, I have had a new melody racing through my mind for some time now and I just can't think of anything else. Let me play it for you and perhaps you can help me with the words."

After kneeling in prayer and clutching her little Bible, the blind poetess stood to her feet with face aglow, saying, "Why, that music says, 'Blessed Assurance, Jesus is mine! O what a foretaste of glory divine...' "

Soon the words began to flow from her heart, and there was born another of more than 8,000 gospel hymns by this godly woman.

Regardless of how a person tries to describe, define, or explain the gospel song, it must be recognized that these simple but emotional expressions have been greatly used by God to promote His message. Critics have attacked them for their inferior literary and musical qualities, and many may deserve criticism. Yet it cannot be denied that these songs have been one of the powerful factors in the spread of the evangelical message.

The Growth of Gospel Music

Five periods in the growth of gospel music may be identified. They are:

1. *Early Gospel Music—1870-1910.* This period was dominated by three individuals: Dwight L. Moody, evangelist; Ira D. Sankey, musician and publisher; and Fanny J. Crosby, blind songwriter.

D.L. Moody. Uneducated and impulsive, he had a magnetic personality. Even though he could not carry a tune, Moody had a high regard for the power of gospel music in the Christian ministry. One of his purposes for starting the Moody Bible Institute in Chicago in 1886 was to train young people for gospel music leadership. In 1893, Daniel P. Towner (1850-1919) was appointed by Moody as the school's first music director. Towner composed the music for numerous gospel songs, including "At Calvary," "Trust and Obey," "Grace Greater Than Our Sin," "Saved by the Blood," "Nor Silver nor Gold," "My Anchor Holds," "Anywhere With Jesus," and "Only a Sinner." Towner trained many notable music leaders, including Charles M. Alexander, Harry Dixon Loes, and George Schuler.

Ira D. Sankey. For nearly 30 years, Sankey worked with Moody as song leader and soloist in his evangelistic crusades. He is often called "the father of the gospel song." Ira Sankey is regarded not only as America's most influential, evangelistic musician, but is also noted for publishing and promoting gospel music. His *Sacred Songs and Solos,* published in England, sold more than 8 million copies. In collaboration with Philip P. Bliss and other gospel musicians, he produced such popular works as *Gospel Hymns and Sacred Songs* (1875), *Gospel Hymns No. 2* (1876), *No. 3* (1878), *No. 4* (1883), *No. 5* (1887), *No. 6* (1892), and the collected *Gospel Hymns, Nos. 1-6* (1894). The royalties from these publications helped finance the campaigns conducted by the Moody-Sankey team.

At first there was much resistance to this new style of sacred music, especially throughout Great Britain. As the meetings progressed in the British Isles, however, Sankey's music became increasingly respected and accepted.

Ira Sankey hymns still sung today include: "The Ninety and Nine," "A Shelter in the Time of Storm," "Trusting Jesus," "Hiding in Thee," "Under His Wings," "For You I Am Praying," and "Faith Is the Victory."

Fanny J. Crosby. Though blinded at 6 weeks of age through

improper medical treatment, Fanny Crosby wrote between 8,000 and 9,000 gospel hymn texts. She has written more loved hymns than any other writer. Ira Sankey remarked that the success of the Moody-Sankey evangelistic crusades was due, more than any other human factor, to the use of Fanny Crosby's hymns. Crosby hymns still sung today include: "Blessed Assurance," "My Savior First of All," "All the Way My Savior Leads Me," "Rescue the Perishing," and "Saved by Grace."

2. *1910-1920.* This decade in gospel music was dominated by the flamboyant evangelist, Billy Sunday, and his genial song leader, Homer Rodeheaver. Under Rodeheaver's leadership, a lively type of gospel song was introduced with words that emphasized personal Christian experience. Billy Sunday's powerful preaching was characterized by his strong denunciations of sin, by the promotion of prohibition, and by converts "walking the sawdust trail." Some of the gospel song favorites of this era were "Brighten the Corner Where You Are," "Sweeter as the Years Go By," and "If Your Heart Keeps Right."

3. *1920-1945.* No national evangelist was prominent during this period. Gospel broadcasting arose during this time. Leading radio preachers were Walter Maier, Charles Fuller, M. R. DeHaan, Paul Radar, and Aimee Semple McPherson. Lively, attractively arranged gospel songs by such persons as Wendell P. Loveless and Merrill Dunlop were featured in these ministries.

4. *1945—mid 1960's.* This era was marked by the rise of such parachurch organizations as Youth for Christ, and by city-wide crusades such as those conducted by the Billy Graham Evangelistic Association. Gospel music was an important factor in these ministries as a means of attracting hearers and of expressing personal faith. Two leading gospel musicians of these years were John M. Peterson and Ralph Carmichael. Simple but catchy gospel choruses and inspiring but easy-to-sing choir cantatas were distinctive features of this era.

5. *Mid—1960's to present.* An explosion of gospel music has taken place in the past 25 years, resulting in a broad divergence of new styles—folk, country, western, southern, and hard and soft rock. One strong influence has been the gospel music of the Charismatic movement. Organizations such as the Gospel Music Association in Nashville, Tennessee, the large Praise Gatherings in

Indianapolis, Indiana, and the annual Christian Artist's Conference held in Estes Park, Colorado, have all done much to promote the growing popularity of gospel music in recent years.

Summary

The 19th century saw the development of a new form of sacred music, the gospel song. It was born in the emotional era known as Romanticism. Great industrial and social changes were taking place in America. The gospel song is also the product of the revivalist spirit of 1850-1900. This new song was clearly intended to invoke a spiritual response, either for personal salvation or for some commitment to the Christian cause. It is the "music of the people." The gospel song has been America's most distinctive contribution in the development of sacred music.

Group Discussion

1. What relationship do you see between the rise of gospel songs and the American social climate?
2. What response do the words "gospel songs" create in your thinking? What are the negative and positive implications of this expression?
3. In what ways do you feel music can be used as a tool for witnessing? Is it possible to use music wrongly in reaching non-Christians?
4. Using your hymnals as an example, discuss the differences in words and music between traditional hymns and gospel songs.
5. Why is it important for a church music ministry to maintain a balance of traditional hymns and gospel songs? Does your church have such a balance? Give suggestions for improvement.
6. Can you share a time when a particular gospel song influenced someone to become a Christian? Or in making some spiritual commitment?

Reflections

Nothing can occur in your life this day that God and you cannot handle together (see Philippians 4:13).   —Unknown

A little faith will bring your soul to heaven, but much faith will bring heaven to your soul.   —D. L. Moody

What worried, wrinkled Christians need most is a faith lift.
          —Unknown

10
THE SONGS OF TODAY:
CONTEMPORARY TRENDS

A General Background of Our Times
The Avant Garde Spirit
The 20th Century Visual Arts
20th Century Music
Rock and Roll
Contemporary Christian Music
Observations
20th Century Gospel Song Favorites:
  "Because He Lives"
  "Majesty"
Summary

Let them give thanks to the Lord for His unfailing love and His wonderful deeds for men, for He satisfies the thirsty and fills the hungry with good things.   Psalm 107:8, 9

A General Background of Our Times

The 20th century may be the most exciting era of all time. Dramatic events, startling growth in knowledge, and great social progress mark our times. This century may be divided into the pre-1950's and the post-1950's. Its trends have influenced the music of the church. To put it in perspective, we will survey the major events of each era.

Important Events of 1900—1950. The major influences of the first half of the 20th century are: powered flight and air travel; the 1917 Communist revolution in Russia; World War I (1914-1918); radio and motion pictures; the Great Depression of the 1930's; World War II and atomic bombs on Japan in 1945; establishment of the United Nations; rise of neoorthodoxy.

Important Events of the post-1950's. The significant trends of the years since 1950 are: television; advances in high technology; Korean War, 1950's; medical advances—antibiotics, transplants, scanners; rise of the Third World countries; fear of nuclear destruction; concern for human rights; minority group struggles; population and environmental concerns; space exploration; Vietnamese war, 1960's; college campus unrest, 1960's; drug abuse; influence of Eastern mystic cultures; sexual freedom; feminist movement; pro-life and the abortion controversy; energy crisis; new Humanist manifestoes; the age of the computer; the electronic church; international terrorism; Liberation Theology; the Charismatic movement; rebirth of conservatism and evangelicalism.

The 20th century has been influenced by a system of philosophy known as *existentialism.* These are its main teachings:

The universe has no purpose or meaning.

Life has no inherent purpose or meaning for the individual.

Existence precedes essence—the acts or experiences of life constitute being. Reality is to be found in the acts of the moment. This gave rise to the "now" ethic.

Influential philosophers whose writings have had a profound effect on the 20th century include:

George Hegel (1770-1831) German. Truth is a continuous process of Thesis-Antithesis-Synthesis. There are no absolutes. Life is an ongoing process toward self-consciousness.

Soren Kierkegaard (1813-1855) Danish. "Christian existentialist." Taught that faith is a "leap into the dark," a pilgrimage into the unknown that ultimately leads to God.

Friedrich Nietzsche (1844-1900) German. Taught that since God is dead, man must create his own moral values.

Jean-Paul Sartre (1905-1880) French. Playwright. Leader of the Existential Movement in France.

Important theologians influenced by existentialism were:

Karl Barth (1886-1968) German.

Paul Tillich (1886-1965) German-American.

Reinhold Niebuhr (1892-1971) American.

These men were early leaders of *Neoorthodoxy.* This movement was a reaction against liberalism, but made the full authority of Scripture dependent upon a person's acceptance of the Bible—"it *becomes* rather than *is* the inerrant Word of God." This contrasts with the traditional orthodox view that God's Word is inspired, whether it is received or rejected.

The Avant-Garde Spirit

One basic quality of 20th century art is that it cannot be content with traditional materials, techniques, and expressions. Art must grow to stay alive. This thinking produced the restless searching for the new and different—the spirit of the avant-garde.

The 20th Century Visual Arts

The 20th century visual arts are characterized by *abstracting* or *fragmentation,* a revolt against literalism and sentimental Romanticism. It includes these forms:

Expressionism—the world of the inner eye. Does not reflect what the artist sees literally, but how he reacts to it emotionally. Example, Vincent Van Gogh (1853-1890).

Cubism—relating all subject matter to geometric forms. Depicts man's search for a higher reality. Example, Paul Cezanne (1839-1906).

Dadaism—an angry, fanatical art. Its slogans are "Destruction is creation" and "All of life is absurd." Example, Marcel Duchamp (1887-1968).

Surrealism—an emphasis on the subconscious and dream associations. Related to Freudian psychology. It depicts the loneliness of 20th century man and the irrationality of life—"all is chance." Example, Salvador Dali (1904-   ).

Abstract Expressionism (Non-objective Art)—arrangements of colors and shapes on a canvas for their own sake, with no intent to recall or evoke any imagery in the real world. Example, Piet Mondrian (1872-1944).

Pop Art—the art of the 1960's to the present. Often depicts the common and banal scenes of everyday life—cigarette butts, toilets, and soup cans. Example, Andy Warhol (1930-1987).

Pablo Picasso (1881-1973) may be the most recognized artist of this century. He was born in Southern Spain, but spent most of his life in France. Picasso worked in nearly all of the contemporary styles.

20th Century Music

While fragmentation and abstraction are the basic features of

20th century art, *atonality* (no tonality) became the ideal of 20th century music. This dissonant sound was developed in the compositions of Arnold Schöenberg (1874-1951) Austrian-American, in a style known as Serial Composition or The Twelve-tone Row of music. The music is based on a composer's use of an arbitrary scale, with all 12 tones of a scale considered exactly equal. Therefore, there is no restful tonal feeling or center. Any combination of notes can be used for a chord, with no distinction made between disharmony and harmony. Therefore, the composer never felt the need to resolve a dissonant sound.

Since the mid-1950's, *electronic music* has become popular. Just as visual artists are experimenting with hi-tech materials and techniques, musicians are experimenting with new sounds through the use of sound generators, synthesizers, and computers. Important names in the field of electronic music have been Karlheinz Stockhausen (1928-   ) German, and Milton Babitt (1916-   ) American.

Representative composers of *serious 20th century music* include: Igor Stravinsky (1882-1971) Russian; Bela Bartok (1881-1945) Hungarian; Vaughan Williams (1872-1953) English; Alban Berg (1885-1935) Austrian; Sergey Prokofiev (1891-1953) Russian; Paul Hindemith (1895-1963) German; Aaron Copland (1900-   ) American; Dmitri Shostakovitch (1960-1975) Russian; Benjamin Britten (1913-1976) English; Charles Ives (1874-1954) American; Leonard Bernstein (1918-   ) American.

Rock and Roll

Since the late 1950's, one of the most powerful influences in today's society has been rock and roll. This musical sound is dominated by electronically amplified instruments, especially guitars. It has a driving rhythmic beat with simple melodies and harmonies. This physical sound controls the listening habits of today's youth. According to a national survey, 87 percent of all teenagers listen to rock music more than 3 hours each day. Today's music business has become one of the world's most lucrative enterprises, with billions spent annually for music, recordings, videos, and electronic equipment. Regardless of our personal assessment of rock and roll, we would probably have to agree with Leonard Bernstein's statement: "Ninety-five percent of this music is likely junk. The other five percent, however, may change the entire future of American music."

Older adults may not appreciate the "racket" of rock music, but they find the words to be the most offensive and controversial. They are often lewd, irreverent, and arrogant—promoting permissive and perverted sexual behavior, the use of drugs, Eastern mysticism, violence, and disrespect for authority. In recent times, non-religious authorities have become increasingly alarmed about the moral effects of many of the rock lyrics. They are asking: "Has rock music gone too far?" Legislation is proposed that would make it mandatory to identify the content of the songs on album covers.

Most young people thoroughly enjoy rock music, however. Its heavy beat is captivating—a welcomed relief from the "rocking chair music" and "syrupy sounds" of the previous generation. The lyrics hit them where they live and think. They feel that the music is free of the hypocrisies and romanticized sentiments of traditional music. *It has been well stated that to understand today's youth, one must begin to understand their music.*

Contemporary Christian Music

The rock sound began to appear in church music in the mid-1960's, and it has grown in popularity and influence. Realizing the impact rock music has on young people, Christian musicians began matching religious lyrics with heavy beat music.

Proponents have justified their actions with these arguments:

1. Why should the devil have all of the appealing music? Let's face it: Christian young people no longer relate to traditional church music. To them it is old-fashioned and irrelevant. To attract and keep the younger generation in our churches, we must use music that appeals to them.

2. Just as we must communicate to individuals in language they understand, so we must present the Scriptures and spiritual truths to our young people in forms they understand. Although biblical truth never changes, the language we use to express that truth changes with each generation. The church must always be willing to change.

3. Christian rock music gives young people a viable alternative to secular rock. It lets them hear a positive message rather than negative values. Because of their rising popularity, Christian rock songs are now being aired on secular rock radio stations.

4. Many young people have professed Christ as Savior through the ministry of contemporary music at Christian rock concerts.

Christian rock music will often give the gospel a hearing with non-Christian young people.

5. Precedents already exist. Christian leaders such as Martin Luther, Charles Wesley, and William Booth of the Salvation Army used the popular music of their day for the texts they wrote. Some of the best-loved hymn tunes of today were originally secular music, such as "A Mighty Fortress Is Our God" and "Amazing Grace."

6. Music itself is neither sacred nor secular. Therefore, no musical style is inherently evil. The words make the difference. Worthy lyrics sanctify a secular melody.

Opponents of using the rock sound in church music respond with these arguments:

1. Christian rock music is a cheap and distorted representation of biblical Christianity. It is too closely allied with the world's lifestyle. A Christian's calling is to be separate from all evil associations. A worthy result never justifies a wrong means.

2. Christian artists who perform this music, though sincere, are using worldly, sensational methods hoping to achieve spiritual results. Their ministry often appears to be a cover-up for commercial exploits.

3. The words of these songs are usually based on experience. They do not express the objective, unchanging truths of God's Word. Popular, "relevant" words may actually be irreverent expressions. Their vague mention of love relationships and commitments could be interpreted as referring to human partners as well as to God.

4. The rock music sound is not compatible with the Christian message because it is intrinsically evil. Dr. Howard Hanson, former director of the Eastman School of Music, seeking to disprove the argument that the music itself is amoral or neutral, has stated: "Music can be soothing or invigorating, ennobling or vulgarizing, philosophical or orgiastic. It has powers for evil as well as good."

5. Christian rock concerts promote an anti-local church attitude. Christian young people only want to be entertained.

6. Rock style singing is harmful to the voice because it does not use proper vocal techniques.

Observations

Without attempting to settle this sensitive controversy "once and for all," let us consider the following observations:

1. The question of appropriate musical styles for the local church has never been more diverse and divisive. Yet this is also "the age of the evangelical." Opportunities for ministering the gospel are available as never before. We must not become so involved with our differences and cultural preferences that we miss these opportunities for representing our Lord and presenting His message to needy individuals.

2. The selection of music for all phases of the church program calls for careful and mature discernment by church leaders. The congregation should be prayerfully involved in this concern as well.

3. The church music director's prime responsibility is to build up spiritually the entire congregation. He is not to entertain, nor is he to crusade for his personal musical preferences.

4. The musical tastes of any congregation are local rather than national. The music ministry in any church must be geared to the cultural background and personal convictions of the mainstream of the congregation. Music that is acceptable in one community may not be in another.

5. The challenge of today's church music leaders is to satisfy the entire congregation without violating scriptural principles. The music ministry should work toward a balance in styles that is God-honoring, true to the Scriptures, and aesthetically satisfying to the majority of the congregation.

6. Sacred music must not be judged as good or bad merely because it is traditional or contemporary. Each song must be evaluated on the basis of its own words and music.

7. Our study of church history has shown us that periods of spiritual renewal have always been accompanied with outbursts of new Christian songs, and that the style for that music has originated outside the church. In time, the "old secular" becomes the "new sacred." That process may be going on today.

8. To some older believers, anything new and unfamiliar is viewed with suspicion. Many younger people, however, feel that anything traditional has lost its value. Neither extreme is valid.

9. Though there are many tensions in church music, there are many positive factors. The young people coming out of our Christian schools are better trained than ever. Numerous church

music conferences and workshops for music leaders are held each year. More churches see the value of a complete music program. A strong creative spirit is prevalent.

10. We are in danger of losing perspective. The ultimate objectives of a church music ministry must always be to glorify God, to present the gospel, to lead believers in worship, and to give them expression for their spiritual experiences.

Two 20th Century Gospel Songs

"Because He Lives"

For the past two decades, the music of Gloria and Bill Gaither has made a deep impact on the music of the church. Such songs as "He Touched Me," "Something Beautiful," "Let's Just Praise The Lord," "The King Is Coming," "There's Something About That Name," and "I Am Loved" are representative of the 400 songs that have flowed from the hearts and pens of this talented couple.

The song "Because He Lives" reflects their own philosophy, "the resurrection principle in the daily routine of life." Bill Gaither recalls the circumstances that prompted the writing of this song.

We wrote "Because He Lives" after a period of time when we had a kind of dry spell and hadn't written any songs for a while...Also at the end of the 1960's, when our country was going through some great turmoil with the height of the drug culture and the whole "God is Dead" theory which was running wild in our country and also at the peak of the Vietnam War, our little son was born,—Benjy—at least Gloria was expecting him. And I can remember at the time we thought, "Brother, this is really a poor time to bring a child into the world." At times we were even quite discouraged by the whole thing. And then Benjy came, and so that lyric came to us, "How sweet to hold our new-born baby and feel the pride and joy he gives, but better still the calm assurance that this child can face uncertain days because Christ lives." And it gave us the courage to say "Because Christ lives we can face tomorrow" and keep our heads high, and hopefully that could be of meaning to other people.

Words by Gloria Gaither (1942-   )
William J. Gaither (1936-   )
Music by William J. Gaither

Majesty

Words and Music by
JACK HAYFORD

So ex - alt, lift up on high the name of

Je - sus. Mag - ni - fy, come glo - ri -

fy Christ Je - sus, the King.

Ma - jes - ty, wor - ship His ma - jes - ty.

Je - sus, who died, now glo - ri - fied, King of all Kings.

"Majesty"

Popular in the past few years is the use of biblical words with a fresh, contemporary musical style. The popularity of these songs has prompted many congregations to use two music books, a traditional hymnal and a collection of these newer choruses. These contemporary songs have brought a freshness and renewal to church services.

A representative of this group is "Majesty." It was written and composed by Jack Hayford, senior pastor of The Church of the Way, Van Nuys, California. He gave the following account of its composition:

> In 1977 my wife and I spent our vacation traveling throughout Britain. It was the same year as Queen Elizabeth's 25th Anniversary of her coronation, and symbols of royalty were abundantly present beyond the usual.
>
> While traveling through many of the castles of the land, I began to sense the influence one might feel if raised as a child in such regal settings.
>
> One day, as Anna and I drove along together, at once the opening lyrics and melody of "Majesty" came to my heart. I asked her to jot the words and the melody line in the notebook she had beside her.
>
> So powerfully did the sense of Christ Jesus' royalty, dignity and majesty fill my heart, I seemed to feel something new of what it meant to be His! The accomplished triumph of His Cross has not only unlocked us from the chains of our own bondage and restored us to fellowship with the Father, but He has also unfolded to us a life of authority over sin and hell and raised us to partnership with Him in His Throne—Now! (Ephesians 2:1-6).
>
> After returning to our home in California, I completed the song, but the Spirit-borne influence bringing the concept so vividly to my soul is as described above.

"Majesty" describes the kingly, lordly, gloriously regal nature of our Savior—but not simply as an objective statement in worship of which He is fully worthy. "Majesty" is also a statement of the fact that our worship, when begotten in spirit and truth, can align us with His Throne in such a way that His Kingdom authority flows to us—to overflow us, free us and channel through us.

He has birthed us into His eternal Kingdom, with dynamic implications for the present and for eternity. We are rescued from death, restored to the inheritance of sons and daughters, qualified for victory in battle against the adversary, and destined for the Throne forever in His presence!

Summary

The 20th century has been marked by an exploding growth of knowledge and technological advancement, but also by intense turmoil and unrest. A restless, avant-garde spirit characterizes much of its artistic expression. *Today's Christians must try to understand the cultural spirit of this age,* however, if they are to minister effectively for Christ. God has called us to represent Him at a difficult, exciting, and challenging point in history. Let it be said of us as it was of the children of Issachar in the Old Testament: ". . .were men who had understanding of the times, to know what Israel ought to do. . ." (1 Chronicles 12:32 KJV).

The evangelical message is more alive today than ever before. Part of this spiritual awareness is reflected in contemporary Christian music, which has attracted a broad response from Christians and non-Christians alike. Yet this music has been a source of tension and controversy. We must learn to differentiate between unchanging biblical principles and our own variable, cultural attitudes. *Musical differences based on cultural preferences alone must never be allowed to divide the family of God.* Let us begin to practice grace toward those whose cultural tastes and practices are different than our own. May we be resolute, however, whenever the gospel is distorted and the integrity of the Scriptures is involved. This epigram by Augustine, the early church theologian, summarizes what our attitude should be:

"Let there be in the essentials, unity.
In all non-essentials, liberty.
In all things, charity."

Group Discussion

1. How is culture—the visual arts, music, drama of the 20th century a reflection of this age?
2. If a Christian earnestly believes that a particular cultural expression is contrary to the Scriptures and harmful to society, what should he do?
3. What is the responsibility of Christian parents when their young

people fill the home with objectionable secular rock music? Discuss the best ways of handling this matter.

4. As a group project, discuss and evaluate a contemporary Christian song. Is this song usable in your church service on the basis of the biblical criteria in Philippians 4:8? Is the music appropriate and enhancing to the text?

5. Share a contemporary gospel song or chorus that is meaningful to you and tell why.

6. What is your response to Christian rock music concerts? What about heavy amplified instruments, spectacular staging techniques, and choreography? Should this be limited to the concert hall, or can it be used in the church services?

7. How can we attract and hold today's young person in this church? How can young people contribute to the services and ministry?

Reflections

Rules without a proper relationship lead to rebellion. Rules with a quality relationship lead to a loving response.   —Unknown

God does not comfort us to make us comfortable, but to make us comforters.   —Unknown

A Charge To Keep I Have

A charge to keep I have—A God to glorify,
Who gave His Son my soul to save and fit it for the sky.

To serve the present age, my calling to fulfill—
O may it all my pow'rs engage to do my Master's will!

Arm me with jealous care, as in Thy sight to live;
And O Thy servant, Lord, prepare a strict account to give!

Help me to watch and pray, and on Thyself rely;
And help me ne'er my trust betray, but press to realms on high.
                            —Charles Wesley (1707-1788)

Prayer

Dear Lord, we are thankful to be alive during these thrilling though difficult times. Give us a greater desire to reach this generation with Your gospel and love. By Your Spirit teach us the proper balance of being in but not of this world. May our personal cultural preferences never cause us to lose the love and acceptance we share with other believers. This is our prayer in Christ's name. AMEN.

11

THE SONG AND THE CHURCH'S MISSION

On this rock I will build *My church,* and the gates of hell will not overcome it.
                                               Matthew 16:18

Develop a Philosophy

What is the role of music in the mission of the church? The next two chapters will propose an answer to this important question by looking at five aspects of the church's ministry:

- Worship
- Evangelism
- Christian Education
- Fellowship
- Social Concern

The final lesson, "The Song Improved," will translate the information, concepts, and convictions of this book into action. Establishing and improving the music program of the church is every member's responsibility. Each member, regardless of musical ability, needs to be involved in the continuing process of evaluation and long-range goal setting. The work of God requires our finest commitment!

His Church

Christ's church can be viewed on three different levels: *the church personal, the church local* and *the church universal.*

The church personal: This label refers to believers who represent Christ in everyday life. They are seeking to reach people at their point of need (spiritual, physical, emotional, social) and directing them to God and into a loving, Bible-centered local church.

> . . .the kingdom of God is within you.　　　—Luke 17:21

> Lord, speak to me, that I may speak in loving echoes of Thy tone. As Thou hast sought, so let me seek Thy erring children lost and lone.　　　—Frances Ridley Havergal

The church local: This term speaks of individual congregations of Christians who realize that they have been chosen of God to accomplish His earthly purposes—to serve as a "spiritual hospital" for hurting humanity—to proclaim this message through word and song with absolute clarity:

> Come to Me, all you who are weary and burdened, and I will give you rest. Take My yoke upon you and learn from Me, for I am gentle and humble in heart, and you will find rest for your souls.　　　—Matthew 11:28, 29

> Earth has no sorrow that heav'n cannot heal.—Thomas Moore

The church universal: The "called out" body of believers in Christ from every age, race, and culture with whom the Savior will share eternity.

> . . .then before me was a great multitude that no one could count, from every nation, tribe, people and language, standing before the throne and in front of the Lamb.—Revelation 7:9

> We'll join the everlasting song, and crown Him Lord of all!
> —Edward Perronet

The promise of Christ is that nothing, not even the gates of hell, will ever triumph over His church. (Matthew 16:18).

The Mission of the Local Church

The first description of a New Testament church is given in Acts 2:41-47. In this Scripture are revealed five purposes for a local church:

1. *The Local Church Worships Together.* They remained true to the Lord in doctrine, fellowship, breaking bread, praying, and praising (vv. 42, 46, 47).

2. *The Local Church Evangelizes Together.* Three thousand people responded to Peter's sermon, were baptized, and were added to the church. Other persons were added daily as they were saved (vv. 41, 47). Their leaders ministered with power and spiritual authority. Reverential awe came upon everyone, and spiritual wonders were demonstrated by the apostles (v. 43).

3. *The Local Church Learns Truth Together.* They remained true to the apostles' doctrine (v. 42).

4. *The Local Church Fellowships Together.* They had all things in common and were strongly unified (vv. 44, 46).

5. *The Local Church Reaches Out Together.* They shared their wealth with those in need (v. 45).

These five purposes, put into practice by the local church at Jerusalem shortly after Pentecost, are still valid guidelines for churches today. In a time when many churches have neglected these spiritual mandates, when they no longer seem effective in reaching the lost, and when many members have become lethargic, *it is imperative for concerned believers to renew their commitment to God's mission through the local church.*

A local church that is committed to its purpose will include these ministries:

1. *Worship for believers.* It will lead in promoting the infinite worth of God with appropriate proclamations of that worth.

2. *Evangelism for unbelievers.* It will proclaim the gospel and urge personal decisions and commitment on a local and worldwide basis.

3. *Instruction for believers.* It will initiate a program of Christian education that provides teaching, discipling, and nurturing for every age group.

4. *Fellowship for all believers.* It will encourage the "body" relationships of caring and sharing in Christian love.

5. *A living representation of God.* It will demonstrate to the community God's concern for the total needs of individuals (Psalm 82:3, 4; Luke 4:18).

Music and the Church's Mission

The music ministry of the local church should help the church accomplish its mission. Every music group and even every song used should be evaluated in the light of these criteria:

1. *Worship and music.* Music heightens our God-consciousness.

Although beauty and worship are not synonymous, there is a strong relationship between our aesthetic and spiritual responses. The strains of the prelude, the singing of the congregation, and the blended sounds of a choir lift the worshiper to fresh awareness of God.

2. *Evangelism and music.* Music prepares the listener for God's Word. Many believers will testify that a particular song has influenced them to trust Christ. Every important evangelistic movement in church history has been accompanied by a revival of sacred song.

3. *Instruction and music.* Music helps us learn spiritual truth. The music and Christian education ministries are closely allied.

4. *Fellowship and music.* Music unifies. Making music together changes people from a collection of individuals into a unit—a congregation, a choir.

5. *Social concern and music.* Music promotes a benevolent spirit. The truths of worthy sacred songs penetrate and motivate our social consciousness. We become people-oriented and better able to minister with acts of mercy to the needs of the whole person.

We must distinguish between sacred music and church music. Sacred music is an art form that meets the aesthetic and artistic demands of quality composition and performance. Church music, however, is a functional art. It serves the purposes of God and His church. Music does not exist for its own sake within the church program. The sanctuary is not a concert hall for the performance of great music. Nor is the church service an occasion for displaying musical talent. Rather, the music ministry is an effective means for the church to achieve its God-given mission. This is not a plea for mediocrity in either the quality or performance of church music. Our sacrifices of praise should always be our best. We dishonor God by anything less. The validity of church music must be judged by whether or not it helps the local congregation glorify God, edify His people, and accomplish its mission.

The Adult Choir*

There are different kinds of gifts, but the same Spirit. There are

---

*See—*Pocket Guide for the Church Choir Member* by Kenneth W. Osbeck, Grand Rapids: Kregel Publications, 1984.
Devotional Warm-Ups for the Church Choir by Kenneth W. Osbeck, Grand Rapids: Kregel Publications, 1985.

different kinds of service, but the same Lord. There are different kinds of working, but the same God works all of them in men. The body is a unit, though it is made up of many parts; and though all its parts are many, they form one body. So it is with Christ.

1 Corinthians 12:4, 5, 6, 12

Every believer has been given at least one spiritual gift to assist the local church in its God-given mission (1 Peter 4:10). The goal of local church leaders is to help each member identify and use his spiritual gift.

Music is not named as one of the spiritual gifts in the New Testament. The gift can be implied, however, because music helps the church achieve its scriptural purposes. The music group that gives the strongest support to the church's mission is the adult choir. The goal of younger church singers should be eventual membership in the senior choir. The adult choir members should be among the most spiritual, loyal, and thoroughly trained of the church's musicians.

An effective adult choir (ideally about ten percent of the active church membership) can make a strong contribution to the ministry of the local church because:

• It offers a more heightened expression of praise to God than can be given by the congregation.
• It provides leadership and support for congregational singing and Scripture readings. It sets the spiritual tone for the entire service, and it complements the proclamation of the written Word.
• It is an example to the congregation of attentive listening to the sermon.
• It demonstrates to the congregation a proper attitude for worship.
    . . .that thou mayest know how thou oughtest to behave thyself in the house of God, which is the church of the living God, the pillar and ground of the truth. —1 Timothy 3:15 (KJV)
• It represents the important New Testament truth of the priesthood of the believer—lay people who are actively involved in the worship and praise of God.
• It supplies the church with a core of people who, because of their position of leadership, should be concerned about their witness and lifestyle.
• It gives individual members an opportunity for unusual spiritual growth, fellowship, and service.

But the adult choir does more than just prepare a song each week. It builds the body of Christ by the use of God-given spiritual gifts. Choir members and music leaders must always view themselves first as ministers and then as musicians. It is a privilege, yes, but it is also a solemn responsibility!

> God sent His singers upon the earth
> With songs of sadness and of mirth,
> That they might touch the hearts of men
> And bring them back to heaven again.
> —Henry Wadsworth Longfellow

Graded Choirs**

...let the little children come to Me, and do not hinder them for the kingdom of God belongs to such as these.   Mark 10:14

The prized possessions of any local church are its children and youth. The teaching and training of the young in the ways of God should be given highest priority. Christ displayed a prime example of this concern. Despite the pressures of ministering to the multitudes, He took the time to invite children to Himself.

Christian leaders have long realized that music is one of the most effective ways of teaching children spiritual truths. Many gospel hymns were written for this specific purpose. The influence of secular music on today's youth is unquestioned. *When music is properly administered in the church, it is one of the best ways in the entire Christian education program to reach and teach children and teenagers.*

Purposes of a Graded Choir Program***

A graded choir program gives every age group the opportunity to minister through music. A graded choir program includes a beginners' choir, ages 4 and 5; a primary choir, grades 1 through 3; and a junior choir, grades 4 through 6. About 50 percent involvement of each age group should be expected. Also, a teen music-dramatic program that includes vocal, instrumental, and dramatic activities should be involved. A vigorous music program

**See—*My Music Workbook* by Kenneth W. Osbeck, Grand Rapids: Kregel Publications, 1982.
A Junior's Praise (Hymnal) by Kenneth W. Osbeck, Grand Rapids: Kregel Publications, 1969.

***See— *The Ministry of Music* (textbook) by Kenneth W. Osbeck, Grand Rapids: Kregel Publications, 1961.

for all ages will contribute to the success of a local church's Christian education and youth ministries.

Benefits of a Graded Choir Program

1. *It perpetuates church music.* If there are to be better trained adult singers and congregations with a greater understanding and appreciation of the music in the church, this training must begin with the young.

2. *It enriches a child's life.* Music is natural and satisfying to most children and youth. The average youngster will enjoy and respond to music that is presented properly.

3. *It ministers spirituality to the child.* A dedicated music director can make a profound impact on a young person. He will seek to lead each youngster to a personal relationship with God, develop concepts of worship, prepare for a lifetime of Christian service, and demonstrate the richness of Christian fellowship.

Summary

Not everyone is musically gifted or able to sing in pitch. Even so, every believer should be given opportunities to respond with joyful sounds to the Lord. Silent Christians become stagnant Christians. A vital music ministry in the local church will create a worshipful and joyous atmosphere that in turn will contribute to the spiritual well-being of the entire congregation.

LET GOD BE GOD.
LET THE CHURCH BE THE CHURCH.
LET THE PEOPLE REJOICE!

Group Discussion

1. Why is it important for Christians to have a biblical, balanced view of the church—personal, local, universal?

2. Is it possible for a local church to be involved in worthy activities that do not relate to the five scriptural purposes listed in Acts 2:41-47?

3. Give specific examples from your own experience of how music relates to each of the scriptural purposes of the local church. Give suggestions for improvement of these purposes in this church.

4. Do you feel there is a place in the church service for concerts—for music purely for its own sake and enjoyment? What is the best way in which this type of artistic music and performance can be used in the church program?

5. How does a Christian discover his spiritual gift?

6. Give suggestions for encouraging more adults to become involved in the ministry of the senior choir.

7. Do you feel that your church has an effective music ministry with its children and teens? Offer suggestions for improvement.

Reflections

The church is not a gallery for the exhibition of eminent Christians, but a school for the education of imperfect ones.

—Henry Ward Beecher

In God's service, our abilities must begin with a humble attitude of availability.

—Unknown

Christ for the World We Sing

Christ for the world! we sing; the world to Christ we bring,
With loving zeal; the poor and they that mourn,
The faint and overborne, sin-sick and sorrow worn,
Whom Christ doth heal.

Christ for the world! we sing; the world to Christ we bring,
With fervent prayer; the wayward and the lost,
By restless passions tossed, redeemed at countless cost
From dark despair.

Christ for the world! we sing; the world to Christ we bring,
With joyful song; the newborn souls whose days,
Reclaimed from error's ways, inspired with hope and praise,
To Christ belong.

—Samuel Wolcott (1813-1886)

Prayer

Dear Lord, thank You that we are members of Your church universal, united with believers from every age and culture. Thank You for the privilege of worshiping and serving You with other believers in this local assembly. Give each of us a more urgent desire to accomplish Your eternal purposes—to proclaim the good news of the gospel. We thank You also for the young people of our church. May we have a greater concern for their spiritual training. This we pray in Christ's name. AMEN.

12
THE SONG'S PRAYER:
"LORD, TEACH US TO WORSHIP!"

Jesus answered, "It is written: 'Worship the Lord your God and serve Him only.'"
                                               Luke 4:8

Learning to worship and praise God should be a believer's lifetime pursuit. It is more than knowledge about the subject. Rather, it is a deepening relationship with one's Lord. Even as the disciples were convinced about the importance of learning more about prayer, may this study cause each of us to say—"Lord, teach us to worship!"

The Importance of Worship
The fundamental command of Scripture is for us to love God with our whole being and to worship and serve Him. Worship brings the believer God's blessing. It reflects the depth of his relationship with God. A shallow spirituality results in shallow worship—for the individual and the church. The reverse is also true: inadequate worship produces weak spiritual living.

In our sinfulness we are inclined to make something or someone other than God Himself the object of worship. Even Jesus was tempted by Satan to worship falsely. Yet Christ responded by stating forcefully the dominant theme of the Old Testament—that God alone must be worshiped and served. There is no other god!

The act of worship implies communion and fellowship. The eternal, infinite God desires communion with us; in turn, we are capable of fellowshiping with the living God. If we are to worship God, we must begin by recognizing who He is. Our concept of Him will continue to expand as we grow in grace and in our knowledge of the Lord (2 Peter 3:18).

This process is illustrated by a child's devotion to his parents. In the earliest years, devotion is based on the parents' ability to fulfill basic needs. By the time a child reaches young adulthood, however, he should be developing a deep love and appreciation of his parents for who and what they are. Spiritually, we too must mature in our understanding of God and in our love relationship with Him. *We must worship God not only for what He is doing in our lives, but above all for who He is—His being, character, and works.*

A Definition of Worship

Trying to define the worship experience is difficult because it is different for everyone. For example, worship is:

• A recognition of the supreme worth of God.

• A love response by redeemed man to God's self-disclosure through creation, the Scriptures, and the incarnation of Christ.

• A personal, adoring attitude toward God, and a desire to obey Him.

• The outpouring of a soul at rest in the presence of the eternal God.

• An occupation, not with my personal needs, or even with life's blessings, but with God Himself.

• A quickening of the conscience by the holiness of God; feeding the mind with the truth of God; purging the imagination by the beauty of God; opening the heart to the love of God; and devoting the will to the purpose of God.

Isaiah saw the Lord and worshiped Him (Isaiah 6). Note the five stages of worship recorded in this passage:

1. Recognition: "I saw the Lord..." (v. 1).
2. Praise: "Holy, Holy, Holy..." (v. 3).
3. Confession: "Woe is me..." (v. 5).
4. Assurance of Pardon: "This has touched your lips... forgiven" (v. 7).

5. Dedication: "Here am I . . ." (v. 8).

The worship service can be compared to a dramatic production with the following participants involved:*

> **The actors:** the congregation, whose responsibility is to please the audience—GOD!
>
> **The audience:** the living God. (Of the 107 references to music in the psalms, 35 directly address God as the audience of worship.)
>
> **The prompters:** the leaders of the service, whose responsibilities are to remind the actors of their lines and to ensure that the spotlight remains on the audience, God, at all times.

The worship service may be viewed as the "dress rehearsal." The real "performance" for the congregation begins when the spiritually-uplifted believer leaves the sanctuary to begin a new week as God's personal representative to the world.

New Testament Principles For Worship

Yet a time is coming and has now come when the *true worshipers will worship the Father in spirit and truth,* for they are the kind of worshipers the Father seeks. John 4:23

The basic principle of New Testament worship is recorded in John 4. Here the Lord confronted a lowly woman from Sychar of Samaria at the point of her need. He first invited her to find the "living water" that alone could provide eternal satisfaction for her longing heart. Then, following the woman's response of faith, the Lord taught her the meaning of true worship. The result was that "many of the Samaritans of that city believed on Him for the saying of the woman, which testified, 'He told me everything that I ever did'" (John 4:39). This is always God's pattern for every individual: salvation, worship and service.

A startling new concept of worship was introduced to the woman of Samaria. The Lord called for worship "in spirit and in truth"—in personal sincerity and simplicity. Worship was no longer to be based on tradition and ritual. Because God is spirit, He must be worshiped by the corresponding faculty in man. Worship, therefore, is a personal soul expression; it is an attitude of mind and heart rather than a physical or tangible act. In the Old Testament, worship was a mandatory response to God's

---

*Adapted from Soren Kierkegaard's *Purity of Heart Is to Will One Thing,* pp. 160-166.

unchanging command. In the New Testament, believers worship not only in obedience to God's unchanging command, but also because they want to do the Father's will. In the Old Testament, man could only approach God through the prescribed rites of the tabernacle or temple. In the New Testament, a person's response to God is immediate and personal. Further, we are instructed that our worship is not limited to a particular place or form, but that each believer's body is the temple of God (1 Corinthians 6:19, 20). The offerings God desires today are spiritual sacrifices from each believer (Romans 12:1; Hebrews 13:15, 16).

We should worship God every day. This should be done both privately and with other believers. Christians are instructed to interact with one another—to "spur one another on toward love and good deeds...let us not give up meeting together..but let us encourage one another—and all the more as you see the day approaching" (Hebrews 10:24, 25). Group worship has this promise of Christ's presence:...."where two or three come together in My name, there am I with them" (Matthew 18:20).

Forms of Worship

I planted the seed, Apollos watered it, *but God made it grow.* So neither he who plants nor he who waters is anything, but only God who makes things grow. The man who plants and the man who waters have one purpose, and each will be rewarded according to his own labor. For we are God's fellow workers...   1 Corinthians 3:6-9

Forms of worship services vary according to the cultural backgrounds, personalities, and traditions of the believers. Some church leaders today feel that true worship is best achieved when it is conducted in a structured, liturgical, and meditative setting. Other believers prefer a more free, spontaneous approach to worship. A variety of worship forms is healthy within the evangelical community. The object of worship must always be God, the One who "makes things grow"—not the form or people involved (Ephesians 4:12-16).

Worship flourishes best in an atmosphere of freedom. "Where the Spirit of the Lord is, there is freedom" (2 Corinthians 3:17). Freedom of spirit, however, must not lead to a haphazardness, irreverence, or confusion. Freedom is not chaos. The worship of the church must assume some outward form. Unity of thought and feeling are achieved through a sense of purpose and direction.

The Scriptures teach that all things should be done decently and in order for the purpose of building up one another (1 Corinthians 14:26, 33, 40).

Regardless of what form is used, a worship service should be a balance of joyful celebration and reverent humility. A meditative atmosphere will enable God's "still small whisper" to be heard. The service should progress so that the congregation is eager to receive instruction from God's Word. Finally, the service should challenge the participant to yield to God's will. The object should be a worthier discipleship.

What joy there is in coming to God's own courts so fair,
Where faithful souls are blooming like lilies in His care!
Outside the world makes merry, unhappy 'mid its toys;
But in God's sanctuary the soul finds heav'nly joys.
—From the Swedish. J. L. Runeberg
—Translated by A. Samuel Wallgren

I rejoiced with those who said to me, "Let us go to the house of the Lord."   —Psalm 122:1

Revitalizing Worship

Enter into His gates with *thanksgiving,* and into His courts with *praise:* be thankful unto Him, and *bless His name.*   Psalm 100:4

One primary function of a local church is to provide a weekly opportunity for meaningful, vibrant worship. Many evangelical churches today are criticized for the mundane quality of their worship services. A church may be adequate in evangelism, Christian education, and fellowship, but still be dull and shallow in leading a congregation in worship.

The major spiritual revivals of the Old Testament (2 Chronicles 7:1-6; Ezra 3:10-13; Nehemiah 12:22-30) and throughout the church age resulted in a revitalizing of worship and praise by God's people. In the past decade, evangelical leaders have expressed a renewed concern for true worship. They realize that their people must become actively and creatively involved in the worship service; they cannot be mere spectators at a religious performance. Furthermore, the conviction is growing that a believer needs to experience a personal encounter with God every time he/she attends a church service. One must not be content with merely listening to church announcements, minor doctrinal issues and treatises, pious platitudes, or personal manifestoes. Only an intimate encounter with the Living God can satisfy the spiritual thirst of the human heart.

There is no set way to arrange the activities of a worship service. Each activity, however, should contribute to the spirit of true worship. Most services include the following elements: expressions of praise and adoration, confession of sin, acceptance by God, instruction from the Scriptures, and a time for the congregational response.

Churches from a liturgical tradition will follow the plan of the lectionary and church calendar. This is a yearly schedule focused on the events of Christ's life and certain observances in the ministry of the church. This church year plan is as follows:

Advent: begins with the fourth Sunday preceding Christmas Eve. The emphasis centers on the Old Testament prophecies, a coming Messiah and the establishment of His earthly kingdom. The traditional church color is purple, symbolic of Messiah's royalty. Many churches observe this time by lighting a new candle each Sunday preceding Christmas.
Christmas: begins with Christmas Eve and extends twelve nights to January fifth. The emphasis is on the birth of Christ. The church color is white.
Epiphany: begins with January sixth and extends to Ash Wednesday, the Wednesday before the sixth Sunday preceding Easter. The emphasis is on the Christ Child revealed to the wise men as a manifestation to the Gentile world. The early events of Christ's life are often taught during Epiphany (Luke 2:52). The church color is green.
Lent: begins with Ash Wednesday and includes forty weekdays and six Sundays preceding Easter. The emphasis is that of spiritual self-examination and rededicated living. The church color for this season is purple. The church color for the Good Friday service is black.
Eastertide: begins with Easter Sunday and extends for fifty days, including Ascension Day, and for seven Sundays, ending with Whitsunday (the Day of Pentecost). The church color is green.
Whitsuntide: begins fifty days after Easter and emphasizes the advent of the Holy Spirit. The Sunday after Whitsunday is known as Trinity Sunday. This entire period, ranging from

eleven to sixteen weeks, ends with the last Sunday in August. The church color is red.

Kingdomtide: begins with the first Sunday in September and extends to the Advent season. Its emphasis is on the work of the church throughout the world. There is no church color for this season, although green is often used.

An awareness of the church year calendar is helpful in planning meaningful worship services. The events and observances throughout the year can provide a balanced biblical teaching. Many evangelical churches have periodic special services such as missionary Sundays, evangelistic outreaches, dedicatory services, baptismal and communion observances, patriotic holidays, Thanksgiving programs, Reformation Day, Christian education, and family day services.

Some church leaders, basing their thinking on scriptural passages such as Psalm 100:4, suggest that worship services should progress in spiritual intensity. Beginning with the giving of *thanks,* they should move to *praise,* and then arrive at true worship— *blessing God's name.*

Thanksgiving: Expressions of personal gratitude for the daily blessings of life such as health and strength. This first level of worship is compared to the outer court in the Old Testament temple, where worshipers made the initial preparation for their worship the purchase of animals for a sacrificial offering.

Praise: Expressions of gratitude to God for His spiritual provisions: salvation, guidance, and eternal home. This second level of worship can be compared to the inner court of the Old Testament, where the worshipers offered their sacrifices.

Worship: True worship is blessing [praising] God's holy name. These are expressions of adoration to God for who He is. This third level of worship is compared to the Holy of Holies, where the High Priest only could enter on behalf of the people. With the sacrificial death of Christ, however, the veil of separation between God and man has been removed (Ephesians 2:14-18). Since Calvary, every believer-priest has been invited to come with confidence directly into God's presence (Hebrews 4:16).

A revitalized worship service will inevitably result in an even *greater use of the music ministry* in the local church. True worship and responsive praise are inseparable!

Suggestions for Leaders of Church Services

May Your priests be clothed with righteousness; may Your saints sing
for joy.   Psalm 132:9

It is tragic but true that God's people could attend a lifetime
of weekly church services and never experience the thrill of
worshiping God in spirit and in truth. For them it is a distasteful
duty to perform or a form of entertainment. Revitalized worship
services begin with renewed leaders, since the congregation always
reflects its leadership. Consider these ten suggestions for leaders
of public church services:

1. Begin the service with a spirit of "holy enthusiasm." Whether
you are a pastor or music director think of yourself as *a worship
leader, a "New Testament Levite."*

2. Develop a worship plan for the year. A staff retreat is an
ideal setting to plan the yearly calendar.

3. Determine a theme for each month and publicize it. You
might want to select a corresponding Scripture verse and a chorus
for each month.

4. Think through each service from beginning to end. Begin
on Monday to prepare the next Sunday's services.

5. Study and read aloud the words of the hymns you plan to
use so that you understand and feel them.

6. Plan an attention-getting beginning for each service. Guard
against stereotypes and cliches.

7. Try to make the entire service come alive. Lead with genuine
warmth and inspiration. Provide variety each week.

8. Get as much input as possible from the staff and from church
members (including young people) for the improvement of the
services.

9. Involve lay people of all ages. Make your people participants,
not spectators.

10. Carefully evaluate the strengths and weaknesses of each
service and determine how it could be improved.

Summary

Worship is the cornerstone of a believer's spiritual life. The
bedrock of the local church is its worship service. All aspects
of the church program are founded here. The function of church
music is to glorify God by providing a vehicle for His people
to worship Him. When believers have truly worshiped, they will

return to their individual responsibilities with the song of the Lord on their lips. Their joyous lifestyle in turn will attract non-believers to the gospel, and the church's song will ring over the earth, even as it will throughout eternity.

Come let us tune our loftiest songs, and raise to Christ our joyous strain; Worship and praise to Him belong, who reigns, and shall forever reign.

Group Discussion

1. What does the term "worship" mean to you? Do you worship God in your daily devotional life?
2. Why is it important for salvation and worship to precede witness and service?
3. In what ways can a church worship service become man-centered rather than God-centered? Identify activities in a service that are often substituted for the worship of God. What elements, do you feel, help create a true sense of worship in a service? Which distract?
4. What benefits does a church worship service provide a believer that individual worship cannot?
5. Share an experience you had of worshiping with a congregation whose form of worship differed from your church. What was your response?
6. What would you most like to have changed in your worship service? Discuss specific suggestions for the improvement of announcements; congregational singing; Scripture reading; prayers; the offering; and interaction with the pastor's sermon.
7. As a group project, prepare an order of service that would actively involve your congregation in the worship and praise of God.

Reflections

It is in the worship experience that our relationship with God is established and sustained.   —Robert Webber

Worship renews the spirit as sleep renews the body.
                                        —Richard Cabot Clarke

Too many Christians worship their work, work at their play, and play at their worship.   —Unknown

O Lord, grant that I may desire Thee, and desiring Thee, seek Thee, and seeking Thee, find Thee, and finding Thee, be satisfied with Thee forever.   —Augustine

O Breath of Life, come sweeping through us, revive Thy church
with life and pow'r;
O Breath of Life, come cleanse, renew us, and fit Thy church
to meet this hour.
Revive us, Lord! Is zeal abating while harvest fields are vast and
white?
Revive us, Lord—the world is waiting! Equip Your church to
spread the light. —Bessie Porter Head

Brethren, We Have Met to Worship

Brethren, we have met to worship and adore the Lord our God;
Will you pray with all your power, while we try to preach the
Word?
All is vain unless the Spirit of the Holy One comes down;
Brethren, pray, and holy manna will be showered all around.

Let us love our God supremely, let us love each other too;
Let us love and pray for sinners till our God makes all things new.
Then He'll call us home to heaven, at His table we'll sit down;
Christ will gird Himself and serve us with sweet manna all around.
—George Atkins (19th Century)

Preparing for a Service of Worship

We enter, not as strangers, but as guests of the living God. Before
the service, use the silence to speak with Him. During the service,
allow the Scriptures and the Holy Spirit to speak to us. Following
the service, let us speak with one another.

Prayer

Dear Lord, we give thanks for the privilege of worshiping You
each week with this body of believers. Help us to realize that we
cannot live on this world's "bread" alone, but that we must be
fed on the eternal truths that come from You and Your written
Word. Give us listening and attentive hearts. Teach us, O Lord,
to truly worship You. This we pray in our Savior's name. AMEN.

13
THE SONG IMPROVED:
EVALUATING AND SETTING GOALS

...one thing I do: Forgetting what is behind and straining toward what is ahead, I press on toward the goal to win the prize for which God has called me heavenward in Christ Jesus. All of us who are mature should take such a view of things. And if on some point you think differently, that too God will make clear to you. Only let us live up to what we have already attained.   Philippians 3:13-16

The Continual Need for Improvement
Every member of a local church is responsible for its improvement. We cannot sidestep our obligation by hiring a staff of leaders to do the work for us. We must therefore be involved in the evaluating and upgrading of our church's effectiveness.

Personal involvement is especially important in the church's music ministry. Too often the task is left to the sole discretion of the pastor, music director, or music committee. Church music must minister to every member, regardless of age, cultural background, or musical talent. If the church is to be spiritually mature, its members must be given opportunities to worship God and to respond to Him with their praise.

Basic Precepts for Improvement

The foundation for the improvement of the music ministry in a local church is found in these statements:

1. The entire church must recognize the importance of the music ministry. Churches that are growing spiritually and in numbers invariably have a music program that ministers to all ages.

2. Every church, regardless of size, can develop an effective music ministry. But the congregation must be willing to pray, plan and become personally involved.

3. The music ministry must not be geared or limited to the musically gifted. One prime responsibility of church music leaders is to meet the needs of the entire congregation.

4. No church music ministry ever "arrives." Some areas will always need to be upgraded. An active, growing church will have a sense of vision for its future (Proverbs 29:18).

5. Church members should be encouraged to express their feelings about the music ministry, and to offer positive, constructive suggestions. When ill feelings are ignored, the congregation will eventually suffer.

6. Church services should be conducted in a manner that represents the congregation's desires and needs. The leadership cannot impose a style that does not meet the people where they are.

Areas of Improvement

Now that you have discussed the material in the preceding lessons and have developed a biblical, historical, and philosophical perspective for church music and worship, it's time to evaluate your church's music ministry. Our aim is to make immediate improvement, if necessary, and to establish worthy long-range goals where needed. Areas for evaluation and goal-setting are:

1. The administration of the music program.
2. Congregational singing.

3. Graded choirs—children's music.
4. Youth-teen music.
5. The Adult Choir.
6. Instrumental music.
7. Music in the home.
8. Encouragement of creativity.
9. Development of accompanists and organists.
10. Development of lay people for congregational song leadership.

The following checklist will help you evaluate the music ministry of your church. This process of evaluation and goal-setting must be conducted with a gracious spirit and in Christian love. Criticism should never be given to hurt someone or to degrade any leader or program. We need a humble, servant attitude as we look constructively at the ministry of this church (Philippians 2:1-5).

1. **Administration**

1. Does your church have a Music Director or Minister of Music? _____ Full Time _____ Part Time _____ Combined with other duties _____ Salaried _____ Voluntary _____
2. Do you have a church music committee? _____ How large? _____ How chosen? (elective/appointed) _____ How often does this committee meet? _____ Does it receive input from the congregation? _____ Does it make positive contributions to the music ministry? _____
3. Do you have an adequate budget for the church music program? _____ How much? _____ Does this include honorariums for special talent? _____ Instrument repair and tunings? _____ Choir robe cleaning and repair? _____
4. Do the pastor, music director, church board, and music committee meet periodically to evaluate the music ministry? _____ To do long-range planning for the Sunday and special services of the church? _____
5. Are the worship services conducted in a mature, creative, enthusiastic manner? _____ Do they promote discipleship within the congregation? _____
6. Is there an evangelistic emphasis throughout the church program? _____ Is the church reaching non-Christian families from the community? _____
7. Does the church use all of its musical potential? _____

8. Does the church have written guidelines for such matters as: Acceptable styles of music to be used in the services? _____ Spiritual qualifications of performers in a service? _____ The use of sound tracks, amplified instruments, choreography in a service? _____ Platform decorum and dress policies? _____ Honorariums for guest performers? _____
9. What areas need immediate improvement in the music ministry in this church? _____
10. List several long-range objectives for the music ministry in this church_____

_____

2. Congregational Singing

1. Is the congregational singing in your services effective? _____ What needs improvement? _____
Name of church hymnal _____
Publisher _____ Date _____
How long has the church used this book? _____
Are you satisfied with the book? _____ Is a "hymn of the month" used? _____ Do you learn new songs? _____ Is instruction ever given about the background of the familiar hymns? _____ Are original songs written by members of the congregation ever used? _____ What accompaniment is generally used for your congregational singing?_____
Is it effective? _____ What type of organ do you have? (pipe, Hammond, Allen, Conn) _____ What kind and what size of piano do you have in the sanctuary? _____
Is it adequate? _____ Are these instruments kept tuned and in good repair? _____ Are the acoustics in the sanctuary adequate? _____ What needs improvement? _____
2. What immediate steps should be taken to improve the congregational singing in this church? _____

_____

3. What are some long-range objectives for improving the congregational singing in this church? _____

_____

3. Graded Choirs—Children's Music

1. Is the music ministry with the children and youth effective? _____ What kinds of music are the children and youth singing in Sunday School?_____
Do you have a children's choir? _____ How many and what age

groups? _____ How many children does this involve?_____ What percentage is this of their Sunday School Department?_____ Do the children enjoy their choir experience? _____ When are the weekly rehearsals held? _____ Is this time convenient for the greatest number of families? _____ Do the rehearsals include instruction (workbooks, notebooks, hymn study) along with preparation for periodic performances? _____ Does your choir get together socially? _____ Do the choirs perform special programs throughout the year? _____ Is the leadership adequate? (director, accompanist, choir mothers and sponsors) _____ Are the rehearsal facilities adequate? (room, chairs, lighting, ventilation, piano, blackboard, bulletin board, phonograph, rhythm instruments)_____

2. What steps should be taken immediately to improve the children's music ministry in this church? _____

_____

3. What long-range objectives should be established for improving the children's music ministry in this church? _____

_____

4. Youth-Teen Music

1. Do you have an effective teenager choir program? _____ What ages does this include? _____ How many teens are involved? _____ What percentage is this of the corresponding Sunday School Departments? _____ Do the young people seem to enjoy their choir experience? _____ When are the weekly rehearsals held? _____ Is this time convenient for the greatest number of families and young people? _____ How often do the young people participate in the Sunday services? _____ Do the young people provide special programs throughout the year? _____ Do they have any evangelistic outreach through music and drama outside of the church? _____ Is the leadership adequate? (director, accompanist, sponsors) _____ Are the rehearsal facilities adequate? _____ Is encouragment given for using individual talent or forming smaller ensembles? _____

2. What immediate steps should be taken to improve the teen music program in this church? _____

_____

3. What long-range objectives should be considered for improving the teen music program in this church? _____

_____

5. The Adult Choir

1. Do you have an adult choir? _____ How large? _____ What percentage is this of the active church membership? _____ How often do they sing in the Sunday services? _____
Do they minister effectively to the majority of the congregation? _____ What kinds of music does the choir sing predominantly? (anthems, hymn and gospel song arrangements, contemporary songs, from the hymnal, a balance of all styles) _____
When are rehearsals held? _____
Is this time convenient for most people? _____ Does the rehearsal include a devotional time to promote the spiritual growth of its members? _____ What are the requirements for membership in the choir? _____
Are these requirements clearly stated in a choir constitution? _____ Does the choir perform special programs throughout the year? _____ Does the choir ever minister outside the church? _____ Is the church music library maintained in good condition? _____ Are the choir robes properly cared for? (storage, cleaning, repairs) _____ Do the choir members seem to enjoy their choir experience? _____
2. Does the choir lead the congregation in a positive worship experience? _____
3. Is the choir's leadership adequate? (director, accompanists, choir officers) _____
4. What immediate steps should be taken to improve the adult choir program in this church? _____
_____
5. What long-range objectives should be considered for improving the adult choir program in this church? _____
_____

6. Instrumental Music

1. Do you have instrumental groups? _____ What kinds? _____ How large? _____ What ages are involved? _____
How often do they perform? _____ When are the weekly rehearsals held? _____ Is this time convenient for most instrumentalists? _____ Are the rehearsal facilities adequate? (room, tuned piano, storage space) _____ Do you have a handbell program in the church? _____ What ages are involved? _____
Is the program effective? _____
2. Is the leadership of the instrumental program adequate? _____

3. What immediate steps should be taken to improve the instrumental program in this church? _____

_____

4. What long-range objectives should be considered for improving the instrumental program in this church? _____

_____

7. **The Home**

Does the church offer any program or give any instruction for the use of music in the home? (family devotions or music workbook projects) _____

8. **The Individual**

Does the church offer any program or give any encouragement to individual creativity? (original writings, stories, poetry, banners, or original sacred songs) _____

9. **Development of Accompanists**

Does the church have a program for developing and scheduling a variety of accompanists, organists, and other individual talent in the services? _____

10. **Development of Lay Song Leaders**

Does the church have a program for training lay people to lead congregational singing? _____ Are trainees given opportunities to lead? _____

What immediate steps could be taken to improve these areas?

_____

_____

What long-range objectives should be considered for improving these areas? _____

_____

Summary

The local church is God's chosen agency for accomplishing His earthly purposes. If the church is to fulfill its scriptural mission, the prayerful concerns and finest efforts of each member are required.

Let us renew our commitment to the cause of Christ as represented in this local congregation, and let us say with conviction:

O Church Triumphant—Sing On! Now and Eternally

Praise the Lord. Praise, O servants of the Lord, praise the name of the Lord. Let the name of the Lord be praised, both now and forevermore. From the rising of the sun to the place where it sets, the name of the Lord is to be praised.   Psalm 113:1-3

Reflections

There is not a heart but has its moments of longing, yearning for something better, nobler, holier than it knows now.

—Henry Ward Beecher

God sends no churches from the skies; out of our hearts they must arise.   —Unknown

God uses ordinary people to accomplish extraordinary feats.

—Unknown

Onward, Christian Soldiers

Like a mighty army moves the Church of God;
Brothers, we are treading where the saints have trod.
We are not divided, all one body we—
One in hope and doctrine, one in charity.

Onward, Christian soldiers, marching as to war,
With the cross of Jesus going on before.

—Sabine Baring-Gould, 1834-1924

Prayer

O Lord God, thank You for the gift of music. I thank You for the spiritual gifts that You have given fellow-believers in this fellowship. Help us to realize that though there are many diverse gifts, we are one Body united in You. Give each of us a greater desire to use our gifts for the continuing improvement of our church's ministry. May the praise and worship of our congregation always glorify You. This we pray in our Savior's name. AMEN.

THE UNFINISHED SONG

A Dramatic Group Reading
adapted from a poem by Annie Johnson Flint

(Three readers and the entire group.)

EVERYONE: "To Him who loves us and has freed us from our sins by His blood, and has made us to be a kingdom and priests to serve his God and Father— to Him be glory and power forever and ever! Amen" (Revelation 1:5, 6).

READER 1: When the heavenly hosts shall gather and the heavenly courts shall ring with the rapture of the ransomed, and the New Song they shall sing; though they come from every nation, every kindred, every race, none can ever learn the music till he knows God's pardoning grace.

READER 2: All those vast eternities to come will never be too long to tell the endless story and to sing the endless song:

GROUP: "UNTO HIM WHO LOVED US AND WHO LOOSED US FROM OUR SINS. . ."

READER 3: We shall finish it in heaven, but 'tis here the words begin.

GROUP: "UNTO HIM WHO LOVED US"

READER 1: We shall sing it o'er and o'er;

GROUP: "UNTO HIM WHO LOVED US"

READER 2: We shall love it more and more;

GROUP: "UNTO HIM WHO LOVED US"

READER 3: Song of songs most sweet and dear;

READER 1: But, if we would know it yonder, we must learn the music here.

READER 2: Here, where there was none to save, none to help us, none to care,

READER 3:   Here, where Jesus came to seek us, lost in darkness and despair,

READER 2:   Here, where on that cross of anguish, He redeemed us from our sins,

READER 3:   Here, where first we knew the Savior, it is here the song begins.

READER 2:   Here, amid the toils and trials of this fleeting earthly life.

READER 3:   Here, amid the din and turmoil of this troubled earthly strife;

READER 2:   Here, in suffering and sorrow, here, in weariness and wrong;

READER 3:   We shall finish it in heaven, but 'tis here we start the song.

GROUP: "UNTO HIM WHO LOVED US"

READER 1:   We must sing it every day,

GROUP: "UNTO HIM WHO LOVED US"

READER 2:   Who is Light and Guide and Way,

GROUP: "UNTO HIM WHO LOVED US"

READER 3:   And who holds us very dear;

READER 1:   If we'd know it over yonder, we must learn the music here.

READER 2:   There will be no silent voices in that ever-blessed throng. There will be no faltering accents in that Hallelujah song;

READER 3:   Like the sound of many waters shall the mighty anthem be, when the Lord's redeemed shall praise Him for the grace that set them free.

READER 1:   But 'tis here the theme is written, it is here we tune our tongue, it is here the first glad notes of joy with stammering lips are sung. It is here the first faint echoes of that chorus reach our ear. We shall finish it in heaven, but our hearts begin it here.

GROUP: "UNTO HIM WHO LOVED US"

READER 1:   To the Lamb for sinners slain;

GROUP: "UNTO HIM WHO LOVED US"

READER 2:   Evermore the joyful strain;

GROUP: "UNTO HIM WHO LOVED US"

READER 3:   Full and strong and sweet and clear;

EVERYONE: BUT, IF WE WOULD KNOW IT YONDER, WE MUST LEARN TO SING IT HERE!

BIBLIOGRAPHY

Allen, Ronald. *Praise! A Matter of Life and Breath*. Nashville: Thomas Nelson Publishers, 1980.

Allen, Ronald, and Borror, Gordon. *Worship: Rediscovering the Missing Jewel*. Portland: Multnomah Press, 1982.

Christensen, James. *Don't Waste Your Time in Worship*. Old Tappan, N.J.: Revell, 1978.

Daniels, Harold M. *What To Do With Sunday Morning*. Philadelphia: Westminster Press, 1979.

Ellsworth, Donald P. *Christian Music in Contemporary Witness*. Grand Rapids: Baker Book House, 1979.

Hustad, Donald P. *Jubilate! Church Music in the Evangelical Tradition*. Carol Stream, IL: Hope Publishing Company, 1981.

Kemper, Frederick W. *Variety for Worship*. St. Louis: Concordia, 1977.

Kendrick, Graham. *Learning to Worship as a Way of Life*. Minneapolis: Bethany House Publishers, 1984.

Lorenz, Ellen Jane. *Glory, Hallelujah!* (The Story of the Camp Meeting Spirituals). Nashville: Abingdon Press, 1978, 1979, 1980.

Lovelace, Austin C., and Rice, William C. *Music and Worship in the Church*. Nashville: Broadman Press, 1976.

MacArthur, John, Jr. *The Ultimate Priority*. Chicago: Moody Press, 1983.

Maxwell, William D. *A History of Christian Worship*. Grand Rapids: Baker Book House, 1982.

Micks, Marianne H. *The Joy of Worship*. Philadelphia: Westminster Press, 1982.

Skudlarek, William. *The Word in Worship*. Nashville: Abingdon Press, 1981.

Taylor, Jack R. *The Hallelujah Factor*. Nashville: Broadman Press, 1983.

Wayland, John T. *Planning Congregational Worship Services*. Nashville: Broadman Press, 1971.

Webber, Robert E. *Worship Is a Verb*. Waco: Word Books, 1985.

_____. *Worship: Old and New*. Grand Rapids: Zondervan Publishing House, 1982.

White, James F. *New Forms of Worship*. Nashville: Abingdon Press, 1971.

OTHER HELPFUL BOOKS

By Kenneth W. Osbeck

DEVOTIONAL WARM-UPS FOR
THE CHURCH CHOIR

Choir directors find this booklet, composed of 43 weekly devotionals for leadership in worship, indispensable for the weekly devotional-rehearsal time.

MY MUSIC WORKBOOK

Provides a basic understanding of reading music, including vocal techniques, hymnbook appreciation, Bible study, worship and instrumental music for the junior age in Christian schools.

101 HYMN STORIES

The true life experiences and touching background stories of 101 favorite hymns are valued for devotions, sermon illustrations, bulletin inserts and historical or biographical research. The music is included.

101 MORE HYMN STORIES

This selection of 101 more hymn stories includes a variety of hymn styles including some 20th century Gospel hymnody and also the older enduring favorites. The music is included.

POCKET GUIDE FOR THE CHURCH
CHOIR MEMBER

A practical booklet of instruction for the individual choir member.

SINGING WITH UNDERSTANDING

Features the hymnal's organization, a sketch of the historical growth of hymnody, varied suggestions to improve the church music program, and hymn backgrounds from 101 Hymn Stories.

THE MINISTRY OF MUSIC

A comprehensive textbook covering the various areas of the church music ministry.

JUNIOR'S PRAISE

100 selected hymns specifically designed to meet the need of the evangelical churches in teaching boys and girls ages 7 to 12 the standard hymns of the faith.